THE UN-KNOWN JAMES DEAN

THE UN-KNOWN JAMES DEAN

ROBERT TANITCH

For Veronica and John Mooney

First published 1997

Printed in Hong Kong
for the publishers
BT Batsford Ltd
583 Fulham Road
London SW6 5BY

ISBN 0 7134 8034 3

Also by Robert Tanitch
A Pictorial Companion to Shakespeare's Plays
Ralph Richardson, A Tribute
Olivier
Leonard Rossiter
Ashcroft
Gielgud
Dirk Bogarde
Guinness
Sean Connery
John Mills
Brando
Clint Eastwood

CONTENTS

Introduction

JAMES DEAN, an actor of outstanding promise, never lived to see his fame, his career tragically cut short almost before it had begun. This book is a pictorial record and chronology of his work in theatre, television and film.

James Dean's fame as an actor rests on three roles: Cal Trask, the bad twin, in John Steinbeck's *East of Eden* (1955), directed by Elia Kazan; Jim Stark, the definitive 1950s teenager, in *Rebel Without a Cause* (1956), directed by Nicholas Ray; and Jett Rink, the cowhand turned megalomaniac tycoon, in Edna Ferber's *Giant* (1957), directed by George Stevens. He was nominated for an Oscar for two out of these three films, but strangely, not for his best performance.

For those who know only of Dean's acting career through these films, it may come as a surprise to learn that between 1951 and 1954 he acted in two major stage roles in New York and in over 30 plays on television, appearing in works by John Drinkwater, William Inge, George Roy Hill, Rod Serling and adaptations of Sherwood Anderson and Henri Bernstein. It is a reminder (if a reminder is needed) that actors do not suddenly appear out of nowhere.

His roles on television tended to be crazy mixed-up kids, teenage delinquents on the run, vagrants, convicts, safe-crackers, counterfeiters and killers, though from time to time he was also cast as a farm boy, a bellhop, a lab assistant, a stevedore and, perhaps more unexpectedly, as a French aristocrat, an apostle and even an angel.

His roles in the theatre included the simpleton in Richard J. Nash's *See The Jaguar* (1952), the homosexual Arab street boy in Ruth and Augustus Goetz's adaptation of André Gide's novel, *The Immoralist* (1954),

and Herakles in a Sunday night reading of Sophocles's *The Women of Trachis* (1954) in a racy translation by Ezra Pound.

Right at the very beginning of his career he landed bit parts in three minor Hollywood movies, playing a GI in Korea in Samuel Fuller's *Fixed Bayonets!* (1951), a boxer's second in the Dean Martin–Jerry Lewis comedy, *Sailor Beware!* (1952), and a young man ordering an ice-cream sundae in *Has Anybody Seen My Gal* (1952).

James Byron Dean, son of Winton and Mildred Dean, was born during the American Depression on 8 February 1931 in Marion, Indiana. The family moved to Los Angeles in 1936 and shortly afterwards his mother died of cervical cancer when she was 29 and he was only 9. Her death left him insecure and vulnerable for the rest of his life. 'What did she expect me to do?' he would ask later. 'Do it all on my own?'

His father, a dental technician, sent him back to Fairmount, Indiana, alone (accompanied by his mother's coffin) to be raised by his aunt and uncle on their 180-acre farm. He saw little of his father thereafter. His aunt was a member of the Women's Christian Union and he learned religious tracts on the evil of drink, which he read to the congregation in the church, his first tentative steps in drama.

At Fairmount High School he was an average student, who was good at athletics and played in the basketball team. He took part in a number of school productions, mainly melodramas, and entered a speech competition, coming first at State level and sixth at the National level. His text was 'The Madman's Manuscript' from Charles

James Dean in
The Immoralist

COSTUME DEPT. PROD. B10
NAME JAMES DEAN
PART CAL TRASK
CHG. # 2 SC. 51-66
EXT. RAIL ROAD YARDS

Dickens's *The Pickwick Papers*.

In 1949 he enrolled in the pre-Law programme at Santa Monica City College, choosing as his subsidiary subject the history of theatre arts. He joined the Jazz Club and Jazz Appreciation Society. He painted the scenery for *The Romance of Scarlet Gulch* at the Miller Playhouse Theater Guild and appeared in the Santa Monica Theater Guild production of *She Was Only A Farmer's Daughter*.

In 1950 he gave up Law and enrolled at the University of California to study Theatre and played Malcolm in Shakespeare's *Macbeth*, his Indiana twang causing much amusement among the students.

In January 1951 he dropped out of university and went to New York and successfully auditioned for The Actors Studio (known to its detractors as 'the slouch and mumble school') becoming one of their youngest members. His idols were Marlon Brando and Montgomery Clift and such was his obsession with both actors that he would sometimes sign his letters James-Brando-Clift-Dean. He took dancing lessons with Katherine Dunham.

James Dean in *East of Eden*

He made his Broadway debut in 1952 in Richard J. Nash's *See The Jaguar* as a simple-minded and bewildered lad who had been locked up in an ice-house all his life. The play was dismissed as sententious and baffling. 'If you want to see *See The Jaguar*,' advised John McClain in *The New York Journal American*, 'you had better hurry.' Theatregoers who did not hurry missed it. The production ran five nights. Dean's notices, however, were excellent (Lee Mortimer, critic of *The New York Daily Mirror*, thought he stole the show) and they led to television engagements.

The early 1950s was the Golden Age of Television in America and drama was one of its staple diets. Dean was one of many young actors who took advantage of the open casting

calls. The teledramas were cheaply made, underrehearsed, poorly designed, flatly lit and crudely staged, but they were an excellent training ground. In the same way that a British actor in the 1950s got his experience in weekly repertory so the New York actor got his experience on television.

His first role was in a religious drama, *Hill Number One*, for Family Theatre ('The family that prays together stays together') in which he was cast as John the Apostle in a retelling of the story of Christ's crucifixion and resurrection.

Between 1952 and 1955 it must have seemed as if he was never off the box, acting opposite such actors as E. G. Marshall (*Sleeping Dogs*), Cloris Leachman (*The Forgotten Children*), Rod Steiger (*The Evil Within*), Gene Lockhart (*The Bells of Cockaigne*), Dorothy Gish and Ed Begley (*Harvest*), Mildred Dunnock (*Padlock*), Eddie Albert (*I'm a Fool*), Mary Astor and Paul Lukas (*The Thief*) and Ronald Reagan (*The Dark, Dark Hour*).

He also worked for such prestigious television series as Omnibus in William Inge's *Glory in the Flower*, which starred Jessica Tandy and Hume Croyn, and Schlitz Playhouse in *The Unlighted Road* in which he was the star.

The shows were live but many of the video tape backups (in case of an emergency on the day of transmission) have been found and these are preserved and can be seen at The Museum of Television and Radio in New York on consoles.

Dean quickly developed a reputation among directors and actors of being difficult to work with. 'I don't see how people stay in the same room with me,' he once said. 'I know I wouldn't tolerate myself.' The complaints were legion: he was ill-mannered, he arrived late, he didn't learn his lines, he didn't stick to the script. He may have been good at improvising on the spot and using the props around him, but he was not so good at finding his marker on the floor and often moved out of the frame. His spontaneity and unpredictably worried and annoyed actors not brought up in the Method school of acting.

In 1954 he was cast as Bachir, the homosexual Arab houseboy in Ruth and Angus Goetz's adaptation of André Gide's *The Immoralist*, starring Geraldine Page and Louis Jourdan. Though the play was perhaps the most serious and outspoken treatment of homosexuality that Broadway had yet seen, the subject was treated so clinically that there was no drama. Dean, however, got excellent reviews, his performance admired for its realistic venality and insidious charm. He left the cast almost immediately after the first night having landed the leading role in Elia Kazan's film version of John Steinbeck's *East of Eden*.

His film debut was an overnight sensation: 'unquestionably the biggest news Hollywood has made in 1955... the screen's most sensational find of the year... the most dynamic star discovery of the year... outstanding talent... the best youngster to hit the screen in years... destined for a blazing career'.

James Dean in *Rebel Without a Cause*

Influential film columnist Louella Parsons guaranteed her readers that 'the twenty-three-year-old actor from Broadway will be the rave of the season.' Her rival Hedda Hopper was not to be outdone: 'I do not remember', she wrote, 'ever having seen a young man with such power, so many facets of expression, so much sheer invention as this actor.'

Cal Trask was a wonderful role for an actor's screen debut. There was hardly a scene in which he did not appear and he was very photogenic. For those who admired his performance, his ability was strikingly in

evidence. He was likened to a captive panther and a young lion and said to have the grace of a tired cat. His good looks, his sensitivity and his dynamism were much commented on. Those who didn't like his performance found him stylized, hard to understand and too much on one note. They saw merely a carboning of Marlon Brando's acting style, personality and mannerisms without Brando's talent and power.

There was hardly a critic who didn't compare Dean with Brando. True, they had been to the same school, the same Method school of acting, The Actors Studio, and Dean had acquired the Method's characteristic vocal and physical mannerisms. But he was nothing like Brando. Brando was 30 and looked it. Dean was 24 and looked like a teenager.

By the time *East of Eden* was released, Brando had appeared in *The Men*, *A Streetcar Named Desire*, *Viva Zapata*, *Julius Caesar*, *The Wild One*, *On the Waterfront*, *Desirée* and *Guys and Dolls*. It is difficult to imagine Dean playing Stanley Kowalski, Zapata, Mark Antony, Terry Malone, Napoleon Bonaparte and Sky Masterton. He would have been the right age for *The Wild One* (righter than Brando at any rate) yet hardly convincing as leader of The Black Rebels' Motor Cycle Club.

Dean's admiration for Brando was well-known but he was understandably irritated by the comparison. 'I have my own personal rebellion,' he was quoted as saying in *Newsweek*. 'I don't have to rely on Brando's.'

Brando was equally irritated: 'I have a great respect for his talent. However, in *East of Eden*, Mr Dean appears to be wearing my last year's wardrobe and using my last year's talent.' Despite the specific reference to *East of Eden*, I suspect his remark was based more on Dean's off-screen behaviour rather than his on-screen performance. It would have been fascinating to see them acting together in

WARNER BROS. STUD[IO]
WARDROBE TEST
FOR
#403 GIANT
OF
JAMES DEAN
AS
JETT

WARDROBE CHANGE # 10
WORN IN { SET INT. BOTTLE
EXT. AIRPO[RT]
EXT.
SCENE 342-36[ ]

 55

Eugene O'Neill's *Long Day's Journey Into Night*, cast as the Tyrone brothers, Dean as consumptive Edmund Tyrone opposite Brando's drunken James.

Originally Kazan had wanted Brando and Montgomery Clift to play the bad and good twins in *East of Eden* but, by the time he had managed to get the production off the ground, they were too old.

Since there were no box office names in *East of Eden*, the film opened to middling business until Dean's death gave the box office the boost it needed. Cal Trask was not, of course, the first of his tortured, inarticulate adolescents – he had already played endless variations on the role on television – but it was the first time the mumbling, the stricken face, the delicate bruised emotions, the upturned eyes, the wrinkled brows, the Kabuki-like knit eyebrows and the hunched shoulders had been seen on the big screen. His vulnerability created enormous empathy. He was not Steinbeck's Cal (though Steinbeck said he was) but rather Dean's Cal. It was an astonishing performance for his first major film.

He was nominated for an Oscar. So were James Cagney in *Love Me or Leave Me*, Frank Sinatra in *The Man with the Golden Arm* and Spencer Tracy in *Bad Day at Black Rock*. They all lost to Ernest Borgnine in *Marty*. Elia Kazan was also nominated for an Oscar and he lost out, too, to Delbert Mann, the director of *Marty*.

East of Eden was the only time Dean got to witness his success. *Rebel Without a Cause* (billed as 'Warner Bros Challenging Drama of Today's Teenage Violence') was premiered four weeks after his death. The film was not only a seminal work on juvenile delinquency but also a damning indictment of parental shortcomings, and as such, it had an obvious appeal to adolescent audiences. Dean became an instant star, an instant symbol of and for

James Dean in *Giant*

disillusioned youth, a prototype rebel, epitomizing every 1950s teenager's frustration and isolation. His affinity with the role was patent and it was the role which would do most to create and perpetuate his image and posthumous myth and cult.

His close relationship with the director, Nicholas Ray, gave him tremendous creative freedom, allowing him to develop his character and even shape the movie itself. No one had previously portrayed the angst, insecurity and bewilderment of youth quite so well. *Rebel Without a Cause* was, perhaps, the first film in which an actor had portrayed a teenager with whom other teenagers the world over could identify. 'Take both your parents to see it', advised one newspaper's headline. The film would be much imitated.

Once again his reviews were excellent: 'a remarkable talent… a player of unusual sensibility and charm… exceptional power and sensitivity… unusually gifted… brilliant… his intensely original performance has the marks of greatness… (and in one silly headline) Not Even Brando Could Equal This'.

His next role was Jett Rink in Edna Ferber's *Giant*, starring Elizabeth Taylor and Rock Hudson, and directed by veteran director George Stevens who (to Dean's undisguised annoyance) did not give him the freedom Kazan and Ray had. Jett Rink was a relatively small part, a supporting role, though important enough for many of Hollywood's leading actors to want to play him. At the premiere, a year after his death, Elizabeth Taylor and Rock Hudson found themselves playing a supporting role to Dean whose every appearance on the screen was greeted with an ovation.

The critics were divided about the film, their evaluations ranging from 'a large and satisfying entertainment' to 'as indigestible as a Texan breakfast of steak, fried eggs and beans'. The critics were also divided about Dean. There were those who thought he was 'great... magnificent... the most brilliant of all the young players Hollywood has discovered since the war... a *tour de force*'. There were many who did not find him great at all. 'Since Dean is dead I shall say nothing about his attempt to portray the mature Jett Rink,' wrote Courtland Phipps in *Films in Review*, 'except to say it is embarrassing to see.' Georges Sadoul went further. Writing in *Les Lettres françaises*, he said Dean had 'descended to third-rate acting'.

The real problem was that he had to age 30 years. Some people were surprised how convincing he was as a middle-aged, power-crazy tycoon; the majority did not find him convincing at all. He was inevitably much more persuasive in the first part of the movie as a young and inarticulate ranchhand. Nevertheless, he was nominated for an Oscar, no doubt because he was dead and no doubt out of respect for the box-office as well. Rock Hudson was also nominated. So were Kirk Douglas in *Lust for Life*, Laurence Olivier in *Richard III* and Yul Brynner in *The King and I*. Brynner got the award.

Apart from acting, Dean's other great obsession was cars and racing. On 30 September 1955, less than two weeks after completing *Giant*, he was driving to Salinas to participate in a race when he was killed in a crash with another car. He was 24 years old.

'Dean's career is not over,' affirmed the Reverend Xen Harvey, officiating at the funeral and getting carried away by the occasion. 'It's only the beginning and remember God is directing the production.'

There had been nothing since the death of Rudolf Valentino in 1929 to equal the mass hysteria which followed. Fans worldwide refused to believe he was dead. There were rumours he was still alive and disfigured in a sanatorium. His homes were ransacked. His Porsche was put on exhibition and dismantled by people wanting souvenirs. Dean became much more famous when he was dead than he had been when he was alive.

For three years after his death he was receiving more letters than any living star. He was widely copied, his image appearing everywhere, on posters, T-shirts, mugs, clocks, even tattooed on people's backs. In the decades which followed he would continue to be seen on hoardings and in commercials helping to sell jeans and banks. Forty years on, he is still in vogue, remembered more vividly than many better actors with far longer careers.

Had he lived he was set to appear on television as the Welsh miner in Emlyn Williams's *The Corn is Green* and in two boxing films, an adaptation of Ernest Hemingway's *The Battler* and *Somebody Up There Likes Me*, the latter the story of Rocky Graziano, played eventually by Paul Newman, who had been a strong contender for *East of Eden*. Nicholas Ray was convinced that, had he lived, he would have discarded acting entirely in favour of directing.

Because Dean died at 24 he remains forever young, immortalized as the ultimate teenage screen hero and rebel. He never had time to destroy his image. He was dead before his hold on the public had weakened. His last film was *Giant*, but his screen epitaph will always be *Rebel Without a Cause*. His best film, however, remains *East of Eden*, which offered him his greatest role and his greatest performance.

The pages which follow are a record of James Dean's work and mercurial talent, his magnetism and charisma, and his enduring and universal appeal across the sexes and age groups.

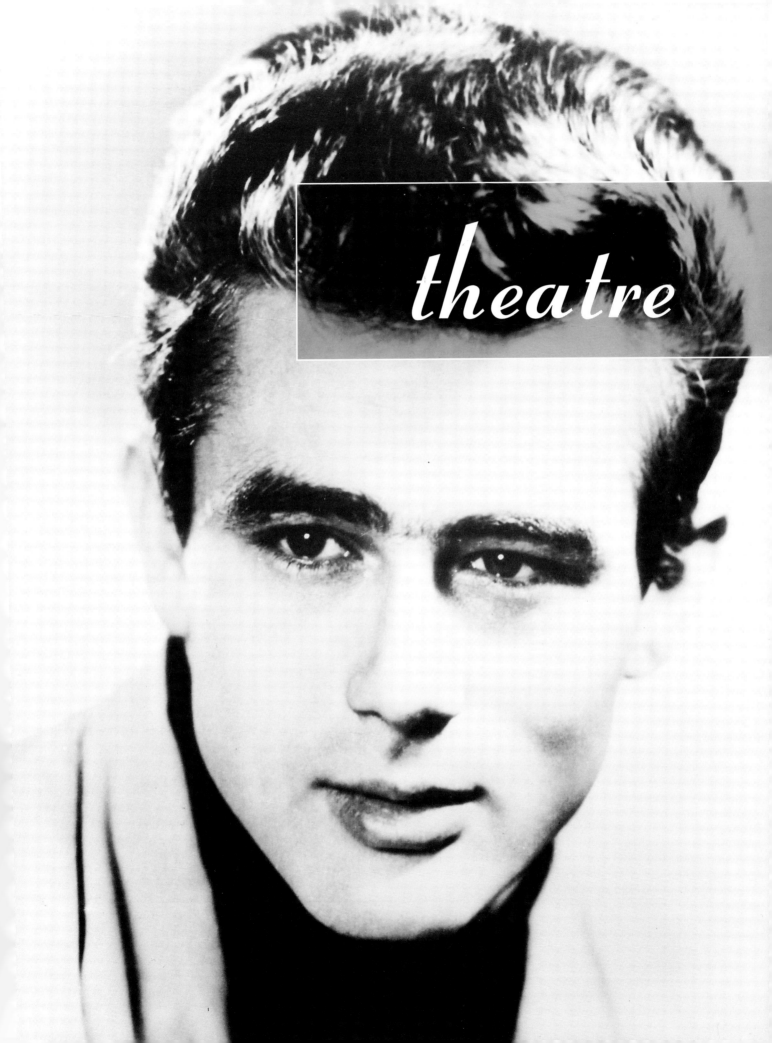

theatre

School Days

James Dean was at Fairmount High School from September 1943 to May 1949 during which time he appeared in a number of school productions. His drama teacher was Adeline Nall, a major influence during his school days.

To Them That Sleep in Darkness

Role   Blind boy
Date   1945

The blind boy regained his sight. The play was performed at the Back Creek Friends Church where his family worshipped.

The Monkey's Paw

Writers   W. W. Jacobs and Lewis N. Parker
Role   Herbert White
Date   1946

The monkey's paw offered its owner three wishes. It was Herbert White who suggested his father should wish for £200 to clear the family debts. He then went off to the factory where he worked and got caught up in the machinery and was mangled to death. The firm offered his parents £200 by way of compensation. Mrs White begged her husband to wish their son alive again. The moment he did, there was a knock at the door and it grew louder and louder and more and more insistent. As she struggled with the door's chain and bolt, Mr White wished his son dead. The knocking stopped instantly. First published in 1902, the story is regarded as one of the best 'three wishes' stories ever written. Dramatized in 1910. it quickly became popular with amateurs with a penchant for the macabre.

James Dean in an unidentified school production

Mooncalf Mugford

Writers   Brainerd Duffield and Helen and Nolan Leary
Role   John Mugford
Date   1947

Mugford was a mad old man who had visions. Thirty-six years later in *Hollywood: The Rebels*, a documentary about Dean, Adeline Nall would recall how, in his enthusiasm for acting, Dean had practically throttled the poor schoolgirl who was playing his wife.

Our Hearts Were Young and Gay

Writers   Cornelia Otis Skinner
          and Emily Kimbrough
Adaptor   Jean Kerr
Role   Otis Skinner
Date   October 1947

The comedy was set in Paris of the 1920s and described the adventures of two unchaperoned 19-year-old girls who were courted by two young Harvard men. Dean played Cornelia Otis Skinner's father, a famous American actor (1851–1942), probably best remembered for the beggar Hajj in *Kismet*.

Goon with the Wind

Roles   Villain and Frankenstein's monster
Date   29 October 1948

Goon with the Wind was an entertainment specially produced for Hallowe'en.

You Can't Take It With You

Writers   Moss Hart and George S. Kaufman
Role   Boris Kalenkhov
Date   1949

The Pulitzer Prize-winning *You Can't Take it with You*, a gentle satire on materialism, preached a folksy message that money wasn't everything. 'Life', said Hart and Kaufman, 'is kind of beautiful if you let it come to you.' The play, first produced in 1936 (and later filmed by Frank Capra with James Stewart) was the perfect antidote for the Depression years. It ran for 837 performances on Broadway. A cast of loveable innocents, eccentrics and dreamers has made it popular with professionals and amateurs ever since.

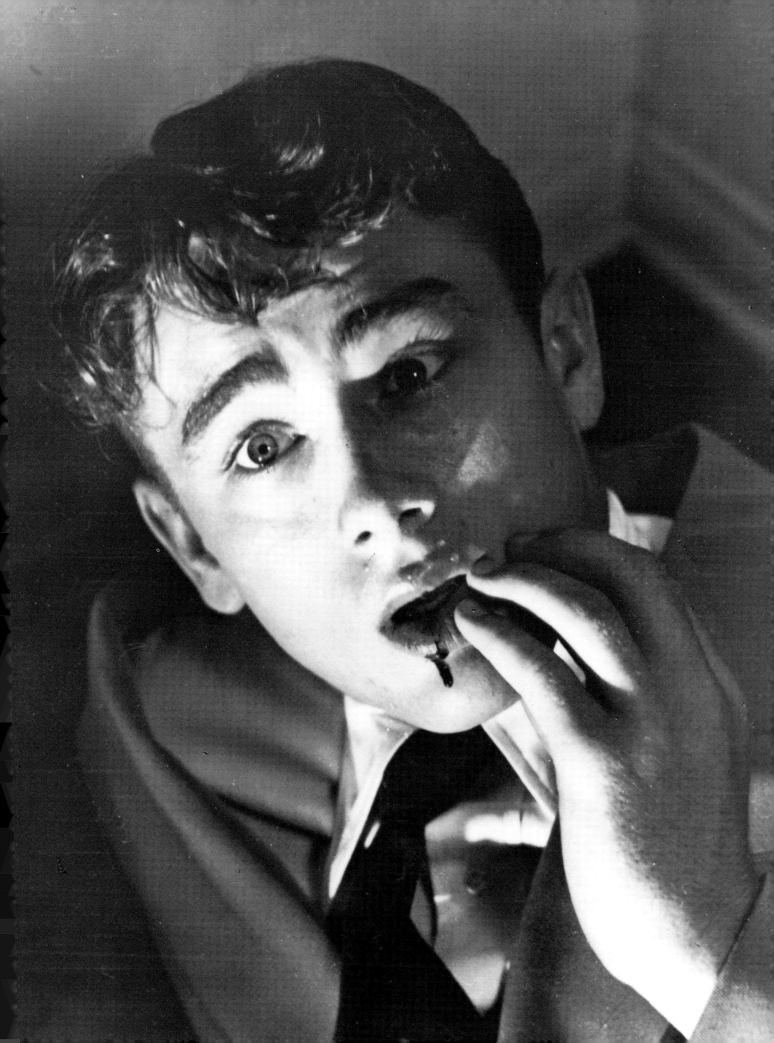

One of the running gags was at the expense of the Russian aristocracy, who having fled the Revolution, were slumming in New York and taking any menial job they could get. Boris Kalenkhov (Dean's role) was a booming, hairy, exuberant, pirouetting, former ballet master who believed 'art is only achieved through perspiration.' He had only one pupil and she had no talent. 'Confidentially,' said Boris, 'she stinks.'

The Madman's Manuscript

Adapted from Charles Dickens's The Pickwick Papers

Role   Madman
Venues   Peru, Indiana; Longmont, Colorado
Dates   April 1949

The manuscript was the purported memoirs of a raving lunatic, who had long believed that hereditary madness existed in his family. He attempted to murder his wife and though he failed, the attempt itself drove her insane and to an early death. Shortly afterwards he successfully strangled her brother.

Dean acted this masterly bit of Grand Guignol (written by Dickens when he was 25 years old) as his entry for the dramatic declamation in the National Forensic League competition. He won first place at state level and sixth place at national level. He might have done even better in the Final had he kept within the time limit laid down by the Board. But, despite having been warned, he refused to cut anything, overran, and paid the penalty. He then had the gall to blame Adeline Nall for his failure.

College and University Days

James Dean was at Santa Monica City College from September 1949 to May 1950 and at the University of California, Los Angeles, from September 1950 to February 1951.

His drama teacher at College was Gene Nielsen Owen. They worked on Shakespeare's *Hamlet* and Edgar Allan Poe's *The Tell-Tale Heart*, the latter no doubt due to his success with Dickens's Madman.

At University he studied the Method with a small group of students under the tuition of actor James Whitmore, a key figure in his development as an actor, and whose help he would always acknowledge. It was Whitmore who recommended he should go to New York.

During this period he was involved in the following productions:

The Romance of Scarlet Gulch

A melodrama with music

Role   Charlie Smooch
Theatre   The Miller Playhouse, Theatre Guild,
            Los Angeles
Dates   August 1949

A Summer Stock production. The action was set during the Californian Gold Rush. Charlie Smooch was a drunk. Dean (billed in the programme as Byron James) also painted the scenery.

She Was Only A Farmer's Daughter

A melodrama by Millard Crosby

Role   Father
Theatre   Santa Monica City College
Dates   May 1950

James Dean in *Macbeth*

Iz Zat So?

A revue

Role   Various
Theatre   Santa Monica City College
Dates   May 1950

Macbeth

A play by William Shakespeare

Role   Malcolm
Director   Walden Boyle
Theatre   Royce Hall, UCLA
Opening   29 November 1950

Malcolm, eldest son of the murdered King Duncan, led a victorious army (famously camouflaged as Birnam Wood) against Macbeth. Harve Bennett, a student at UCLA, writing in the university's Theatre Arts newsletter, *Spotlight*, said that 'Dean had failed to show any growth and would have made a hollow king.'

William Bast, also a student, and later his friend and biographer, thought it was the worst performance he had ever seen and that Dean had no chance of an acting career whatsoever.

The Actors Studio

" After months of auditioning I am very proud to announce that I am a member of The Actors Studio. The greatest school of theatre. It houses great people like Marlon Brando, Julie Harris, Arthur Kennedy, Elia Kazan, Mildred Dunnock, Kevin McCarthy, Monty Clift, June Havoc and on and on and on. Very few get into it, and it's absolutely free. It's the best thing that can happen to an actor. I am one of the youngest to belong. If I can keep up and nothing interferes with my progress, one of these days I might be able to contribute something to the world.

James Dean in a letter to his uncle and aunt

The Actors Studio was a New York-based workshop for professional actors founded by Elia Kazan, Cheryl Crawford and Robert Lewis. Lee Strasberg was the artistic director from 1951 to 1982.

The Studio was not a school and it was very difficult to get into; but once an actor was accepted as a member, he was a member for life. Here actors studied the Method, an introspective approach to acting based on Stanislavsky. The aim was to create a character from within through improvisation. The school's mumblings, hesitations and naturalistic business were made famous by Marlon Brando in Elia Kazan's stage and film productions of Tennessee Williams's *A Streetcar Named Desire* and *On the Waterfront*.

James Dean became a member in 1952 and over the next two years appeared in a number of productions and staged readings on Broadway, Off-Broadway and in in-house performances at The Studio.

Matador

Adapted from a novel by Barnaby Conrod

Role   Matador
Venue   The Actors Studio
Date   1952

The actors in class had to perform a piece in front of their fellow students. Using only a handful of props – a statue of the Virgin Mary, a candle, and a matador's cape – Dean showed the matador preparing for his final bullfight.

" His work provoked a long and penetrating critique from Strasberg. Dean listened impassively, but the colour drained from his face. When Strasberg had concluded his remarks, the young actor slung his matador's cape over his shoulder and silently walked out of the room.

David Garfield *A Player's Place*

The Metamorphosis

Adapted from the novel by **Franz Kafka**

Theatre   Village Theatre, Off-Broadway

Date   August 1952

A man woke one morning to find himself transformed in bed into a gigantic insect. Dean took part in this staged reading of Kafka's nightmare.

End as a Man

A play by by **Calder Willingham**

Director   Jack Garfein

Theatre   The Actors Studio

Date   May and June 1953

Role	Cast
Jocko de Paris	Ben Gazzara
Robert Marquales	William Smithers
General Draughton	Frank M. Thomas
Roger Gatt	Albert Salmi
Harold Koble	Pat Hingle
Maurice Maynall Simmons	Arthur Storch
Perrin McKee	Paul Richards
Starkson	Anthony Franciosa
Larrence Corger	Mark Richman
First Orderly	Al Mifelow
Second Orderly	Richard Vogel
Cadet Officers	Steven Ross, Eli Rill, Richard Hym

End as a Man, a harsh and shocking picture of life in a Southern military academy, was based on Calder Willingham's novel and his own experience in the army.

The cadets were all under the heel of the savagely sadistic Jocko de Paris, played by Ben Gazzara, who would go on to recreate the role in the 1957 film, also known as *The Strong One*.

Dean appeared in the third act trial as a cadet officer, resplendent in his dress uniform, gold-braid cap and red sash, sitting at a table taking notes, a walk-on part.

The production (initially performed for just three in-house performances) transferred first to Off-Broadway at Theatre de Lys in September and then to Broadway at the Vanderbilt Theater, with the above cast but without Dean, who had other commitments. He had landed a small but important role on television in William Inge's *Glory in the Flower* opposite Jessica Tandy, who had created Blanche DuBois in Tennesse Williams's *A Streetcar Named Desire* on Broadway in 1947.

The Seagull

A play by **Anton Chekhov**

Role   Konstantin Treplev

Venue   The Actors Studio

Date   1953

When Chekhov was asked how he would like his play performed he replied he would like it performed as well as possible. Konstantin, short story writer and would-be expressionistic playwright, attempted to commit suicide and succeeded at the second attempt. The production was an in-house performance.

Aria Da Capo

A play by **Edna St Vincent Millay**

Role   Pierrot

Director   Fred Stewart

Venue   The Actors Studio

Date   1953

Aria Da Capo, a short, poetic antiwar play, first performed in 1919, became popular again after World War II. The title refers to a song in three parts and reflected the play's structure. The action was framed by a harlequinade. Two lovers, Pierrot and Columbine, flirted in the most affected and silly manner while two shepherds built a wall between their respective lands, an action which led to a quarrel which ended with them killing each other. This production was also in-house.

The Scarecrow

A play by Percy MacKaye

Theatre	Theatre de Lys
Date	16 June 1953.

Director	Frank Corsaro
Designers	William and Jean Eckart
Music	Joseph Liebling
Costumes	Ruth Morley
Producers	Terese Hayden, Liska March

Role	Cast
Goody Rickby	Patricia Neal
Dickon	Eli Wallach
Rachel Merton	Anne Jackson
Ebenezer	Milton Carney
Richard Talbot	Bradford Dillman
Justice Gilead Merton	Milton Selzer
Lord Ravensbane	Douglas Watson
Mistress Cynthia Merton	Mary Bell
Captain Bugby	Albert Salmi
Minister Dodge	Alan MacAteer
Mistress Dodge	Zita Rieth
Sir Charles Reddington	Harold Preston
Mistress Reddington	Sybil Baker
Amelia Reddington	Eavan O'Connor
Rev Master Rand	Milton Carney
Rev Master Todd	Ed Williams
Micah	Stefan Gierash

The Scarecrow or *The Glass of Truth*, a satire on witchcraft, superstition and bigotry set in colonial America during the late seventeenth century, was based on Nathaniel Hawthorne's *Feathertop*.

Percy MacKaye's play, first acted at Harvard University in 1909 and popular with amateurs and college students in America (no doubt on account of its large cast) had not had a commercial revival since its failure in New York in 1911 when it ran for 23 performances. The critics were divided as to whether it was worth reviving.

Dickon (a Yankee version of the Devil) transformed a scarecrow into a man called Lord Ravensbane so that he could take his revenge on Justice Merton who was about to get married to Goody Rickby. Unfortunately for Dickon, Ravensbane fell in love with her, developed a conscience, and killed himself so that she could marry the man of her choice.

Dean had the non-speaking role of the scarecrow's mirror image, a role so small he did not get a programme credit.

James Dean attends dance classes given by Katharine Dunham in New York

See The Jaguar

A play by N. Richard Nash

Theatre	Cort Theatre, New York*
Date	6 December 1952
Director	Michael Gordon
Scenery	Lemuel Ayres
Costumes	Lemuel Ayres
Music	Alec Wilder
Producers	Lemuel Ayres with Helen Jacobson

Role	Cast
Hilltop	Phillip Pine
Yetter	David Clarke
Janna	Constance Ford
Gramfa Ricks	Roy Fant
Mrs Wilkins	Margaret Barker
Dave Ricks	Arthur Kennedy
Brad	Cameron Prud'Homme
Harvey	George Tyne
Frank	Arthur Batanides
Meeker	Ted Jacques
Mrs Meeker	Florence Sundstrom
Wally Wilkins	James Dean
Jee Jee	Dane Knell
Sam	Harrison Dowd
Andy	Harry Bergman
Carson	Tony Kraber

*See The Jaguar was also seen at Parson's Theater, New Haven, Connecticut, and at Forrest Theater, Philadelphia, in November 1952 prior to its New York premiere.

Constance Ford, James Dean and Arthur Kennedy in *See The Jaguar*

Advance publicity described *See The Jaguar* as an allegorical Western without a horse. Seventeen-year-old Wally Wilkins (James Dean) had been locked up in an ice-house since childhood. His paranoid mother had wanted to protect him from the meanness of the world. Just before her death she released him. Guileless and innocent, he prowled the mountainside looking for her, his eyes opened for the first time to a world of beauty and brutality. He was given shelter by a kind schoolteacher (Arthur Kennedy) and his pregnant partner (Constance Ford).

Wally killed a jaguar and was imprisoned in a cage by the local sheriff (Cameron Prud'Homme), who owned all the land and intimidated everybody on it. The sheriff had intended to add the jaguar to his collection of caged animals which he used as tourist bait at the gas station/store he ran. The teacher set Wally free and the sheriff shot the teacher.

The critics praised the acting but didn't care for the play, finding it verbose and pretentious, and the symbolism obscure and confusing.

❝ James Dean, making his Broadway stage debut, is overwhelming as the boy brought from the icehouse into a world incomprehensible to him.

Whitney Bolton Morning Telegraph

❝ James Dean achieves the feat of making the childish young fugitive believable and unembarrassing.

Richard Watts Jr New York Post

❝ James Dean acted the mentally retarded boy with sweetness and naivete that made his torture singularly poignant.

George Freedley Morning Telegraph

❝ James Dean adds an extraordinary performance in an almost impossible role.

Walter F. Kerr New York Herald Tribune

❝ James Dean is gently awkward as the ignorant boy.

William Hawkins New York World–Telegram and Sun

❝ As the boy, James Dean is very good.

John Chapman New York Daily News

The Immoralist

A play by **Ruth** and **Augustus Goetz** adapted from the
book by **André Gide**

Theatre   Royale Theatre, New York*
Opening   8 February 1954*

Director   Daniel Mann*
Settings   George Jenkins
Costumes   Motley
Lighting   Abe Feder
Producer   Billy Rose

Role	Cast
Marceline	Geraldine Page
Dr Robert	John Heldabrand
Bocage	Charles Dingle
Michel	Louis Jourdan
Bachir	James Dean
Dr Garrin	Paul Huber
Sidma	Adelaide Klein
Moktar	David J. Stewart
Dolit	Bill Gunn

Geraldine Page and
James Dean in
The Immoralist

The Immoralist opened out of town at
Forrest Theater, Philadelphia, directed by
Herman Shumlin, followed by a week of
previews in New York from 1–7 February.

The year was 1900. A young French
archeologist, intent on putting his past behind
him, impulsively married the most respected
woman in the Normandy village where he
lived. They honeymooned in Biskra, North
Africa. She could not understand his coldness
to her until he confessed he was homosexual.
She took to the bottle.

James Dean (his blond hair dyed and
heavily made up to look brown) played the
Arab houseboy Bachir, an insolent, lazy, lying,
thieving, blackmailing pervert, who offered his
services to the soldiers at the local barracks
and was always on the look-out for rich
tourists to ensnare and make his fortune. It
was he who seduced the archeologist with his

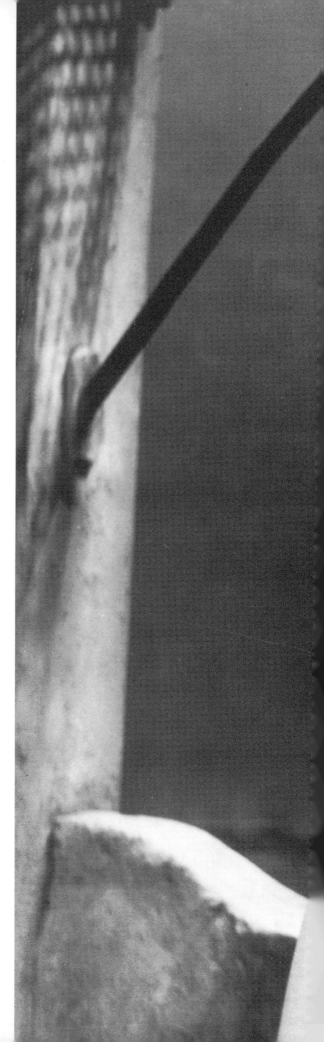

rhythmic dancing whilst snipping a pair of scissors. 'The first time I saw you, I know what you are. It's no secret.' Dean wore a long, loose burnoose and his sexual gyrations were much commented on.

Louis Jourdan (making his Broadway debut) and Geraldine Page got better notices than the play. The main objection was that it was neither a fair adaptation of André Gide's semi-autobiographical novel, nor good theatre. The writing was criticized for being far too reticent and skirting the issues it raised. The theatrical profession described the production as a 'nervous hit' (i.e. nobody was quite certain whether it would succeed at the box office). In the event it ran for 104 performances.

The Immoralist was, in fact, far more up-front (and therefore less commercial) than *Tea and Sympathy*, Sherwood Anderson's matinee play, produced in 1953 and still running, which told the story of a schoolboy (John Kerr) falsely accused of having sex with a schoolmaster and the kind housemaster's wife (Deborah Kerr, no relation) who offered him tea and her bed.

James Dean was one of 12 actors who won a Daniel Blum Theater World Award for Promising Personality of 1953/4. Other winners were Ben Gazzara and Harry Belafonte.

Winners in previous years had included Marlon Brando, Burt Lancaster, Patricia Neal, Carol Channing, Julie Harris, Charlton Heston, Grace Kelly, Richard Burton, Audrey Hepburn, Geraldine Page and Paul Newman.

66 It is James Dean as the houseboy who clearly and originally underlines the sleazy impertinence and the amoral opportunism which the husband must combat.

William Hawkins *New York World–Telegram and Sun*

66 Note the insidious charm of James Dean as an idle native boy.

Brooks Atkinson *New York Times*

66 James Dean makes a colorfully insinuating scapegrace.

Walter F. Kerr *New York Herald Tribune*

66 James Dean is realistically unpleasant.

Richard Watts Jr *New York Post*

66 James Dean is sly and rascally as a roguish and blackmailing houseboy.

Thomas R. Dash *Women's Wear Weekly*

66 James Dean gives the best masculine performance in the role of the Arab boy, a part which could so easily have become extremely offensive with less good acting and direction.

George Freedley *Morning Telegraph*

66 At the play's final curtain one is left with the impression that Michael is a homosexual living ahead of its time and that at some later date in the history of civilization it will be possible for the abnormal to live undisguised and unapologetic within our society... You may not be be very touched by *The Immoralist* but, thanks to the validity, you will not soon forget the questions it touches upon.

Henry Hewes *Saturday Review*

Women of Trachis

A play by **Sophocles**, translated by **Ezra Pound**

Theatre   Cherry Lane
Date   12 February 1954

Director   Howard Sackler
Music   Leonard Rosenman

Cast
Anne Jackson / Eli Wallach
James Dean / Adelaide Klein
Earle Montgomery / Joseph Sullivan

The Cherry Lane Theatre was at the New School of Social Research. Howard Sackler's production was a staged reading of of Sophocles' tragedy, *Trachiniae*, translated by Ezra Pound whilst he was still incarcerated in St Elizabeth's Hospital. His version was no respectful translation, but a startling, free-swinging, very free-swinging, slangy adaptation, switching from stark drama to humour and back again, often in mid-speech.

James Dean was cast as Hyllus, son of Herakles and Daianeira played by Eli Wallach and Anne Jackson. Hyllus denounced his mother for murdering his father – 'Damn you, I wish you were dead' – and bitterly reproached the gods for their pitiless treatment of his dad.

❝ A series of Sunday night dramatic readings got off to a fine start. Eli Wallach, Anne Jackson, Maureen Stapleton, Alfred Ryder and James Dean, to name the outstanding ones, were those performing in the past weekend's program – a double bill of Euripides' *Electra* and Sophocles' *Trachiniae*.

Brooklyn Daily Eagle

Maureen Stapleton and Alfred Ryder appeared in *Electra* in a translation by Gilbert Murray.

❝ I was introduced to him by the director, Howard Sackler, who referred to him as 'a tough kids who sleeps on nails'. I didn't see him again for about a week and suddenly one night he came to my house. I didn't recognize him. He rang the doorbell and appeared in a motorcycle outfit, black leather. He looked like a member of the Gestapo. He introduced himself and asked if I would teach him the piano. He was a lazy student but a good student, musical and talented. He couldn't really understand why he couldn't play large works by Beethoven and Mozart without practice.

Leonard Rosenman in interview in *James Dean, The First American Teenager*

Rosenman was commissioned to write the score for *East of Eden* and *Rebel Without a Cause*. He and Dean became good friends.

James Dean in
The Unlighted Road

television

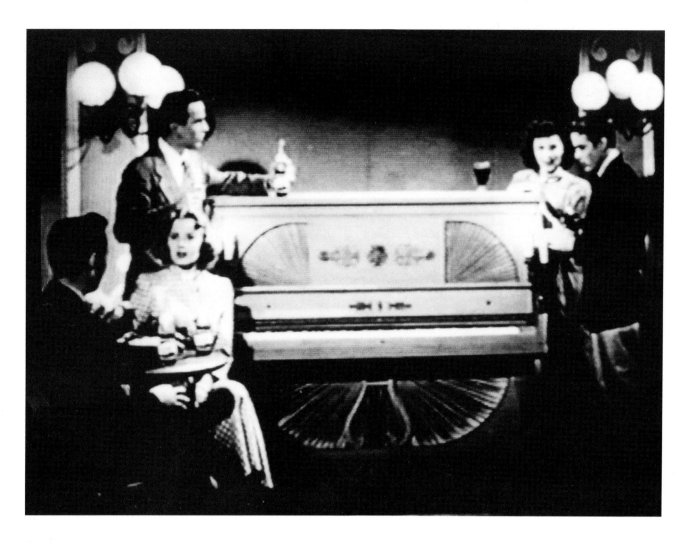

James Dean in
Pepsi-Cola commercial

Pepsi-Cola Commercial

Company   Pepsi-Cola
Network   National
Date   13 December 1950
Producer   Jerry Fairbanks

The 19-year-old James Dean was chosen for the commercial because he looked like a typical American teenager.

The advertisement was in three parts. In the first, a handful of college students were standing round a juke-box. Dean, dressed in blazer and white flannels, put a coin in the machine and then, pressing his ear close to hear if anything was happening and finding nothing was, he gave the piano a big slap. The jingle started ('Go, go, get Pepsi for the Pepsi bounce') and a delighted Dean smiled, clapped his hands and snapped his fingers. Everybody started dancing.

In the second segment the students were still jiving away but there was no sign of Dean. In the final section the boys were seen with their backs to the camera, all huddled together. They parted to reveal a girl carrying a tray of Pepsi cans. Dean was on the far right of the screen and you had to be very quick to catch him, so quickly was he out of the frame.

Hill Number One

Series	Family Theater
Network	National
Date	25 March 1951
Writer	James D. Roche
Director	Arthur Pierson
Producer	Father Patrick Peyton

Role	Cast
Mary	Ruth Hussey
Claudia	Joan Leslie
Matthew	Gene Lockhart
Mary Magdalen	Jeanne Cagney
Pilate	Leif Erickson
Nicodemus	Regis Toomey
Cassius	Henry Brandon
Joseph	Nelson Leigh
Padre	Gordon Oliver
Huntington	Roddy McDowall
Peter	Charles Meredith
Alexander	Frank Wilcox
Flaccus	Everett Glass
Decius	Michael Ansara
Gallicus	Peter Mamakos
Andrew	David Young
John the Apostle	James Dean

Hill Number One was a religious drama, a one-hour Easter television special, reaching an estimated 42, 000,000 viewers. The action was set during the Korean War. An American army chaplain, arriving at the front with coffee for the men, found that their morale was at a low ebb. The GIs wanted to know if there was any meaning to bombarding a hill.

The chaplain decided the best way to buck them all up was to tell them the story of a man who had taken one hill all on his own. The hill, he said, was called Calvary. The story of Christ's crucifixion and resurrection was then re-enacted in flashback. The message, as Father Patrick Peyton explained at the end, was that 'There's a hill in every man's life, but he needn't climb it alone.'

The production, acted by a cast of some 50 actors, was played out in tacky sets. The makeshift costumes looked as if they had come out of a school wardrobe. The dialogue and performances were stilted, anachronistic and in some instances unintentionally funny.

James Dean was cast as John the Apostle.

James Dean in
Hill Number One

He had but two scenes. In the first he was discovered sitting at a table in his jellaba. He was a small, clean-shaven, serious-looking young man; and he looked even younger and smaller, surrounded as he was by big, burly, bearded apostles, all American football-playing types.

John was described by his fellow apostles as timid yet strong. His strength was shown the moment Andrew suggested that the disciples should return to Gallilea. Shocked, he rose to his feet to lecture his elders in a husky voice: 'Surely, we did not spend three years following the Master to return again to our nets? Was it for this the Master sent us to cure the sick, cast out devils?'

Following the crucifixion, the apostles discovered that the stone which had blocked the entrance to the tomb had been rolled away. Dean (now in flowing Arab headdress which made him look very sheikh) had a few more lines: 'He will enlighten us, Peter. Come, we must spread these good tidings quickly. Andrew, Rejoice, He has risen as He promised.'

The girls at Immaculate Heart School in Los Angeles were so moved by the sincerity and the spirituality of his performance that they immediately formed a James Dean Club.

David Young and James Dean in Hill Number One

66 As a record of the Resurrection, it is a moving spectacle with strong appeal for old and young alike. Performed by seasoned actors and of high technical quality, *Hill Number One*, to be accorded its rightful place in Hollywood TV production, need admit no superior.

Daily Variety

T.K.O.

Series	Bigelow Theater
Network	DuMont
Date	29 October 1951
Writer	Ted Thomas
Director	Frank Woodruff
Producer	Frank Woodruff

Cast

Regis Toomey / Martin Milner / Jack Bernardi
John Galludet / Carey Loftin / Jimmy Dundee
Natalie Schaefer / Jeffrey Silver / Mary Jane Saunders
Sarah Spencer / Donald Erickson / Donald Bellis
James Dean / Norman Evans / Noble Chrissel

T.K.O. (technical knock-out) was the story of a teenager (Martin Milner) who became a boxer to raise money for his father's operation while concealing from him and his family that he was a boxer. The story, according to *Variety*, was a technical knock-out. Dean had a small, unidentified role.

Beat the Clock

Series	Game Show
Network	CBS
Date	November 1951
Devisors	Frank Wayne, Bob Howard
Producers	Mark Goodson, Bill Todman

Beat the Clock, the long-running game show, invited members of the public to do silly and almost invariably messy stunts within a time limit of usually one minute. The rules of the game stipulated that the stunts, however bizarre and inane they might be, had to be physically possible. So each stunt was tried out backstage before the show went on air to make certain it wasn't either too hard or too easy.

The show engaged unemployed actors to carry out the tests. They earned $5.00 an hour. One of the actors was James Dean. According to television producer Franklin Heller, he got the sack because he was too good at it. He could do all the stunts.

Into the Valley

Series	CBS Television Workshop
Network	CBS
Date	27 January 1952
Writer	Mel Goldberg
Story	John Hersey
Director	Curt Conway
Producer	Norris Houghton

Cast

James Dean / George Tyne / Robert Baines
Michael Higgins / John Compton

Into the Valley was a jungle warfare drama based on war correspondent John Hersey's account of his first action on Guadalcanal. Dean played one of the dogfaces.

Sleeping Dogs

Series	The Web
Network	CBS
Date	20 February 1952
Writer	Marie Baumer
Director	Lela Swift
Producer	Franklin Heller

Cast

James Dean / Anne Jackson / E. G. Marshall
Robert Simon / Nancy Cushman

The Web was an anthology of dramatizations depicting the plight of ordinary people caught up in sudden and dangerous situations. It was the first television series to win the Edgar Allan Poe Award for suspense stories during the 1951/2 season. In *Sleeping Dogs*, Dean was cast as a vagrant trying to solve his brother's murder.

" He was an absolute horror until we got him on air.

Franklin Heller in conversation at a seminar at
The Museum of Television and Radio, New York

Ten Thousand Horses Singing

Series	Westinghouse Studio One
Network	CBS
Date	3 March 1952

Writer	Worthington Minor
Story	Robert Carson
Director	Paul Nickell
Producer	Worthington Minor

Role	Cast
Marv Payne	John Forsythe
D. D. Dillward	Catherine McLeod
Bullets Riordan	Joe Morass
Mr Caslan	Grady Sutton
Mr Racknall	Vaughn Taylor
Mrs Racknall	Rita Morley
Henry Bascomb	Casey Allen
Bellhop	James Dean

James Dean was barely on the screen before he was off. He appeared right at the very beginning, cast as a bellhop riding in a lift to the tenth floor. He was seen in profile and had just one line ('Ten, please') addressed to the elevator man.

He staggered out of the elevator carrying the luggage of a quarrelling couple. A hotel guest (John Forsythe) came to the rescue of the woman (Catherine McLeod) who was being molested. 'You're not supposed to drag girls into hotel rooms, not unless they want to be dragged,' he said. The molester (Vaughn Taylor) took off his spectacles and punched him on the jaw.

The cameraman just about caught Dean screwing up his face (in the bottom right hand corner of the frame), a reaction shot to the blow which was happening off-screen.

The Foggy, Foggy Dew

Series	Lux Video Theater
Network	CBS
Date	17 March 1952

Writer	J. Albert Hirsch
Director	Richard Goode
Producer	Cal Kuhl

Role	Cast
Kyle	James Dean
Man	James Barton
Mrs McCallum	Muriel Kirkland
Mr McCallum	Richard Bishop

Young Kyle, a happy teenager (not the sort of role Dean was usually offered) had been brought up by foster parents. On a hunting trip he met his biological father, a strange looking drifter with a guitar. The man recognized his son. The foster parents begged him not to tell Kyle that he was adopted. And he didn't.

Prologue to Glory

Series	Kraft Television Theater
Network	NBC
Date	21 May 1952

Writer	E. P. Conkle
Director	n/a
Producer	n/a

Role	Cast
Abraham Lincoln	Thomas Coley
Ann Rutledge	Pat Breslin
Grandma Rutledge	Una O'Connor
Denny	James Dean

Kraft Foods was one of the major supporters of live television and Kraft Television Theater was one of television's most prestigious showcases. The series was a Wednesday night institution, winning top ratings and many awards. *Prologue to Glory* described some early episodes in the life of the young Abraham Lincoln, including his clerkship in New Salem, Illinois, his first attempt at politics, his romance with Ann Rutledge, his grief at her death, and his legal examination at Springfield. Dean played Denny, a friend of the future President.

Abraham Lincoln

Series	Westinghouse Studio One
Network	CBS
Date	26 May 1952
Writer	John Drinkwater
Adaptor	David Shaw
Director	Paul Nickell
Producer	Donald Davis with
	Dorothy Matthews

Role	Cast
Abraham Lincoln	Robert Pastene
Mary Lincoln	Judith Evelyn
Hook	Harry Townes
Mrs Stowe	Betty Low
Jennings	Noll Leslie
Samuel Stone	Frank Overton
Susan Deddington	Jean Adair
William Seward	Charles Egelston
James Macintosh	Robert McQueeney
Mrs Otherly	Katherine Raht
Timothy Cuffney	Harold McGee
Clerk	John Buckwalter
William Scott	James Dean
Elias Price	Anthony Grey

Abraham Lincoln, first performed in 1918, was John Drinkwater's best play and he scored a big success with it on both sides of the Atlantic. The action traced the four years from the President's nomination in 1860 to his death in 1865.

Dean was cast as William Scott, a young farm boy, who had been court-martialled and sentenced to be shot at daybreak before the decisive battle which would end the Civil War. Scott's crime had been to fall asleep at his post. He had just completed a 23 mile march and had volunteered for double guard duty to relieve a sick friend.

Lincoln, who was visiting the front at the time, pardoned him. As he said, 'I don't see it's going to do him any good to be shot.' Drinkwater said he had been inspired to write the incident after reading the President's

dictum: 'Must I shoot the simple-minded soldier boy who deserts while I must not touch a hair of a wily agitator who induces him to desert?'

Dean had only the one scene, and it was a much better scene than the one in the play. Frightened, wide-eyed, deathly pale, and barely looking at Lincoln, he broke down unable to stop sobbing, his head resting on the table, and was amazed when he was discharged and sent back to his regiment. He raised his hand in salute. Lincoln offered him his hand.

Much later, when the war was over, and just as the President and his wife were about to leave for the theatre to see Tom Taylor's farce, *Our American Cousin*, Lincoln was shattered to receive a letter from Scott's widowed mother ('a simple farm woman with not much education') thanking him for saving her son's life and telling him that he had been killed in the final battle.

Paul Nickell's production, unlike the play, stopped at this point, obviously feeling that an American audience would know what happened next and the dramatic irony would be all the sharper if the President's assassination were left to the audience's imagination.

Dean's performance, subdued and simple, was totally without affectation. He looked like a boy soldier straight out of an old photograph by Civil War photographer Matthew Brady.

66 Against the stolid figure in black, his performance is visceral enough to draw gasps from viewers at the museum.

David Dalton *Village Voice*

The Forgotten Children

Series	Hallmark Cards Hall of Fame
Network	NBC
Date	2 June 1952
Writer	Agnes Echkardt
Director	William Corrigan
Producer	William Corrigan

Role	Cast
Martha Berry	Cloris Leachman
Pa Carpenter	Elliott Sullivan
Reverend Dennis	Don McHenry
Ingaby Carpenter	Nancy Malone
Delia Brice	Barbara Bolton
Wesley Mitchell	Lee Lindsey
Ma Carpenter	Helen Marcy
Bradford	James Dean
Melanie	Shirley Standlee
Talbot Carpenter	Steve Pluta
Joshua	Larry Newton

The Forgotten Children, introduced by Sarah Churchill (actress daughter of Winston Churchill), was a typical production from Hallmark Cards Hall of Fame, a series which concentrated on acts of courage in people's lives.

This particular story was about Martha Berry, the American philanthropist (1866–1942), one of the outstanding educators of her day, who had devoted her life to the teaching of impoverished children of the mountain regions of the Deep South.

Dean appeared in the opening scene, which was set in the Berry mansion in Georgia in 1887. He was discovered sitting on a stately white pillard porch, cast as an insensitive Southern aristocrat. Dressed in evening attire, wearing a flowery white shirt, bow-tie and white gloves, he scoffed at the very idea of Martha working for a living.

'I'm an emancipated woman,' she declared.

'The only emancipated woman I ever knew lived in a side street in Memphis,' he replied.

'Well, Bradford,' said one of the other ladies on the porch, 'that remark's not very proper.' Nor was it very likely, either, in that period, in the company of well-brought-up ladies.

There was only one other shot of Dean and that showed him manhandling a hill girl whom he had found trespassing and calling her 'trash' and 'a little savage'.

66 In live television you have to conform to a technique. Jimmy didn't want to deal with boundaries. He had a tendency to cross the line.

Nancy Malone in conversation at a seminar at The Museum of Television and Radio, New York

The Hound of Heaven

Series	The Kate Smith Show
Network	NBC
Date	15 January 1953
Writer	Earl Hamner Jr
Director	Alan Neuman
Producer	n/a

Role	Cast
Hyder Simpson	John Carradine
Angel	James Dean
Gatekeeper	Edgar Stehli

Hyder Simpson and his hound dog Rip were at the gates of Heaven. The Gatekeeper informed him that dogs weren't allowed. Hyder refused to enter without Rip. While he was contemplating what to do next a young angel (James Dean) came along and told him that he had made a mistake and he wasn't at the pearly gates of Heaven at all but at the gates of Hell. Rip hadn't been allowed in because he would have known the difference.

The Case of the Watchful Dog

Series Treasury Men in Action
Network NBC
Date 29 January 1953

Writer Albert Aley
Director Daniel Petrie
Producer Robert Sloane

Cast

Graham Denton /James Dean
Dorothy Elder / Thom Carney
John C. Becher /Biff Elliott

Treasury Men in Action was a series of crime dramas based on the files of the United States Customs and Treasury Departments. The moral each week was that in the fight against the criminal classes (smugglers, counterfeiters, gun-runners, illicit distillers, tax evaders, etc.) the government always won. The government liked the series very much.

Dean was cast as a gun-carrying delinquent, the son of one such moonshiner. The Federal agents were able to trace him through a motor vehicle, a hot-rod, he had used when he was delivering the illegal alcohol.

The Killing of Jesse James

Series You Are There
Network CBS
Date 8 February 1953

Writer Leslie Slate
Director Sidney Lumet
Producer Charles W. Russell

Cast

James Dean / John Kerr
Helen Warnow / Addison Powell
James Whitfield / Carl Frank

You Are There was an anthology of major historical events brought to life through re-enactment and interviews. The series was hosted by Walter Cronkite.

The Missouri Law Enforcement Agency finally caught up with Jesse James on 3 April 1882. John Kerr played the legendary outlaw. James Dean was cast as Bob Ford, the man who shot him in the back. The show was aired on Dean's 22nd birthday.

No Room

Series Danger
Network CBS
Date 14 April 1953

Writer Mary Stern
Director n/a
Producer n/a

Cast

Martin Kingsley / Irene Vernon
James Dean / Kate Smith

Danger was a popular series which dealt in murder mysteries, suspense stories and psychological dramas. In this particular episode Dean was cast as a safe-cracker whose elder brother, an electrician, managed to stop him getting involved in a burglary.

The Case of the Sawed-Off Shotgun

Series   Treasury Men in Action
Network   NBC
Date   16 April 1953

Writer   Albert Aley
Director   David Pressman
Producer   Everett Rosenthall

Cast

James Dean / Coe Norton
Joseph Downing / Anita Anton
Humphrey Davis / Ben Gazzara

The Case of the Sawed-Off Shotgun was another drama based on the files of the United States Customs and Treasury Department. The lesson, as always, was that crime didn't pay.

Arbie Ferris (James Dean) was a young hoodlum, who had graduated from a reform school and wanted to emulate his gangster idol. He stole a gun from a bootlegger, Blackie Bowman (Joseph Downing). In the failed robbery which followed he left behind a slim clue by which the Alcohol Unit of the Treasury Department was able to identify and apprehend Blackie.

Ben Gazzara was cast as a good boy trying to persuade Arbie to attend the meetings at the local Boys' Club.

The Evil Within

Series   Tales of Tomorrow
Network   ABC
Date   1 May 1953

Writer   Manya Starr
Director   Don Medford
Producer   Mort Abrahams

Cast

Margaret Phillips / Rod Steiger
James Dean

Tales of Tomorrow was an anthology of Science Fiction stories and stories of the supernatural.

After three years hard work, a research scientist (Rod Steiger) had produced the perfect serum. He brought it home because the laboratory refrigerator had broken down and put it in his own refrigerator. A likely story.

The serum (which released the evil within a human being) was accidentally consumed by his wife (Margaret Phillips), when it spilt on a pie she was eating. She liked her new evil self so much that she burned the precious formula and poured the serum down the drain. Fed up with staying at home and being neglected, she insisted her husband give up his career. He wasn't that keen. 'The whole thing is my life!' screamed Steiger, over-reacting (and over-acting.) He and Phillips seemed to be performing in different plays and there was absolutely no tension when she started brandishing a knife.

The Evil Within offered a rare opportunity of seeing Dean in spectacles on the screen. He was very short-sighted in real life and wore glasses all the time. He was cast as a lab assistant, all buttoned up in a white coat. He had two scenes. In the first there wasn't much for him to do except say his lines, suck his pencil, push his specs back, and not bump into the furniture. In the second scene there was even less to do. He was just a voice at the other end of the telephone telling his boss that the serum would wear off.

66 He would do anything you wanted him to do, but he would never be able to repeat the same moment… He was a very natural actor who didn't know how to separate physical acting from the role itself.

Don Medford in conversation at a seminar at
The Museum of Television and Radio, New York

Something for an Empty Briefcase

Series	Campbell Soundstage
Network	NBC
Date	17 July 1953
Writer	S. Lee Pogostin
Director	Don Medford
Producer	Martin Horrell

Role	Cast
Joe	James Dean
Noli	Susan Douglas
Mickey	Don Hanmer
Mr Sloane	Robert Middleton

The play began with a voice-over: 'Buy the book Joe buys, the book that can change your life.'

Joe Adams, a young, foolish and out-of-work 22-year-old, who had been in prison for four months for petty larceny, sat on the steps of a tenement building and confided in a mate. 'I want to do something,' he said. 'I want to be something so that I can hold my head up. I want to carry a briefcase.'

He decided he would do just one final little job for himself rather than for the crime boss he used to work for. He picked on a poor defenceless girl in the street (a cheaply made and most unconvincing street); but instead of robbing her, he fell in love with her.

Her name was Noli and Noli had ambitions to be a ballerina. Her chance of realizing her ambition seemed pretty remote. Cute, loose-limbed Joe, sexually ambiguous in his black pullover and tight-fitting trousers, looked as if he would have far more chance of becoming a chorus boy.

Noli from Ohio was a Christian. ('Oh, that's wild!' Joe cried in an affected manner.) She accused him of being a philistine and he asked her to spell it. Later he called at her home where she was practising dancing to a

recording of *The Marriage of Figaro*. He lolled against her front door, conscious of his sexuality. He was carrying a briefcase but, as he explained, he had nothing to put inside it.

Joe confessed he was a thief. 'DON'T LAUGH. I'M SERIOUS. THAT'S ALL I AM. THAT'S ALL I'VE EVER BEEN. I WANT YOU TO KNOW THE TRUTH.' He spoke in capital letters, but he kissed her in lower case.

'I didn't mean to do that.'

'I'm glad you kissed me.'

The music on the soundtrack started to get all romantic and gooey and it looked as if they might start dancing at any minute. 'What does philistine mean?' he asked. She lent him her dictionary. He put the dictionary in his briefcase.

In his next scene he was lying on top of a big brass bedstead, wanting to give up larceny and go straight. A big fat slob entered, smoking a big fat cigar. He was the crime boss, Mr Sloane. 'I want to go straight,' said Joe. 'I want to do something worthwhile.' Sloane, unimpressed, threw his drink all over him and gave him a good drubbing. Joe agreed to do one more job. The scene ended with him clutching the briefcase to his chest, a symbol of his desire for a new life of respectability.

In the following scene he was still lying on top of the bed and listening to music. When Noli telephoned, he told her he felt different and that he had bought a dictionary and the other book she had recommended. Sloane turned up in the middle of the call. When Joe refused to go with him, he got another beating, off-screen, but which the viewer was able to half-observe in the reflection of a mirror.

'So long lover-boy!' said his former boss.

Dean staggered and stumbled all over the set, bumping into the furniture (the wash-basin very nearly came off the wall) before he finally picked up his new book just as Noli was entering the room.

Joe now had the three most important things in his life: a dictionary, a girl and a Bible. He felt he was in heaven. As *Variety* was quick to point out, *Something for an Empty Briefcase* belonged to the Dead End Kids school of literature.

66 With such an unbelievable story content and a casting choice for the male lead that was confusing it would have taken more than an elaborate street setting and the other scenes switches to bring forth a telling production. Neither the dialog nor the thinking was the end result of a 22-year-older who had previously made no attempt to leave the life of petty gangdom. His muggery and repetitive hand gesturing were on the ludicrous side, if their intent was to show the sensitivity and groping of the suddenly awakened thief.

Rose *Variety*

Sentence of Death

Series	Westinghouse Studio One Summer Theater
Network	CBS
Date	17 August 1953
Writer	Adrian Spies
Story	Thomas Walsh
Director	Matt Harlib
Producer	John Haggott

Role	Cast
Paul Cochran	Gene Lyons
Ellen Morrison	Betsy Palmer
MacReynolds	Ralph Dunn
Joe Palica	James Dean
Mrs Sawyer	Virginia Vincent
Tommy	Tony Bickley
Mr Sawyer	Fred Scollay
Mr Krantz	Henry Sharpe
Mrs Krantz	Edna Heineman
Lugash	Charles Mendick
The Man	Barnet Biro

Westinghouse was the studio which had brought Reginald Rose's *Twelve Angry Men* to the small screen. *Sentence of Death* was not in the same class.

Ellen Morrison, an outrageous flirt and 'dizzy darling', who was always being featured in the tabloid press, was on the telephone in a drug store when she learned that she had invited ten people to dinner and forgotten all about it. She was just about to get them all over to the store when the owner was shot dead.

At a police line-up the hysterical widow and a silly middle-aged married couple identified Joe Palica as the murderer. ('They're crazy!' he screamed.) Ellen refused to be pressurized by the police into corroborating their evidence, knowing that the man she had seen had been tall and dark.

Much later, after Palica had been tried, convicted and sentenced to the electric chair (events which all took place off-screen) she was sitting in a bar when she saw the murderer. She telephoned the police. They didn't believe her. But she kept going back to the bar, hoping the murderer would turn up again; and it was no surprise when he finally did.

Initially, Palica had been naive, and cocky with it: 'Well, it's not that they can do anything to me. If you're innocent, you're innocent!' Cross-examined by the police (in the Brobdignagian bullfrog shape of actor Ralph Dunn) he admitted to being a 'jerk kid' who didn't like his old man, that he had stolen a car, and been on parole for five years. His face lit up only once when when he was describing how he had taken his girlfriend to a penny arcade.

There was a lot of Method acting going on in Dean's performance. He didn't stop fidgeting, playing with a lighter on the table, turning the scene almost into an audition piece. The police were not impressed. 'You're it!' said Dunn, typecast as solid cop typing away at his typewriter.

'NO!' pleaded Joe. It was obvious to everybody, except of course Bullfrog, that Palica was telling the truth. He could hardly have looked more innocent. Dean was cast in his familiar role of little boy lost in a world of big men, the 'poor sap' you couldn't help feeling sorry for.

While he was in prison, waiting to be electrocuted (a six week wait), he was visited by a more sympathetic policeman (Paul Cochran). 'I'm getting fat,' he said, trying unsuccessfully to laugh away his tears, his hopes of release having just been raised only to be immediately dashed. His haggard face crumbled in close-up. Always quick to respond to emotional scenes, Dean made a tearful exit.

There was a private joke for friends and fellow actors when he (who was rarely seen either on or off-screen without a cigarette dangling from his mouth) had to reject the offer of a cigarette. 'That's a funny thing,' said Palica, 'I never did pick up the habit.'

Sentence of Death wasn't really about him. It was about the growing friendship between a rich and irresponsible woman and a nice and presumably poor cop, an unlikely pairing, and clearly doomed to failure. Palica's role was to bring them together.

Death Is My Neighbor

Series	Danger
Network	CBS
Date	25 August 1953
Writer	Frank Gregory
Director	John Peyser
Producer	Franklin Heller

Role	Cast
Mr Clemens	Walter Hampden
Netta	Betsy Palmer
JB	James Dean
Walter	Frank Martin
Detective	Andrew Duggan
Policeman	Richard Bull

Mr Clemens, who had been the superintendent of an apartment block for the previous 15 years, was about to get the sack. He didn't know it because JB, his boss's young nephew (and whom he was teaching the ropes) hadn't had the heart to give him his notice and eviction orders. He learned his fate from a a new tenant, a glamourous cover girl called Netta, who posed for detective magazines, and was a friend of the boss. She wanted his rooms.

Netta, waggling her bottom at JB, put a record on her portable gramophone and invited him to dance. They danced cheek to cheek, crotch to crotch. JB, not unnaturally, got all horny and thought she was fair game.

'Let's try it again!'

Netta turned off the gramophone.

'Don't turn it off. We've just got started.'

He grabbed her. She showed him the door.

'Don't give me that basic English bit like you're superior or something. You like it.'

She was saved from further advances by the arrival of her boy friend.

Later he went back to her room when she wasn't there to play a record. He was just about to start jerking himself off when Clemens entered and he dropped the gramophone, breaking it. JB, who was on parole, was frightened Netta would report him to the police. Next day he apologised to her for his behaviour and pleaded on Clemens's behalf ('He's a really nice old guy') and made another pass. She slapped his face and threatened to call the police.

Clemens's hobby was collecting true life murder stories and he had 50 years of newspaper cuttings in his filing cabinets. He didn't like Netta, either. 'Some people might do something,' he said ominously. 'We've read enough papers to know what some people might do in a situation like this.'

There was only one thing for the rejected and frustrated JB to do (after he had clutched one of her records to his chest and broken it) and that was to gas her.

He was lying on his bed in his vest, looking at a girly magazine, when the police entered and accused him of attempted murder. JB tried to frame Clemens but the police easily trapped him into a confession.

'What can I say?' he whined. 'I was all mixed-up. I hated her for what she wanted to do to you and because she treated me like I was... like... I was all mixed-up. I didn't know what I was doing.'

JB went blubbing off to prison. Clemens kept his job. He had a good cry, too, feeling that he had just lived one of the headlines in his filing cabinet.

Dean, in his jeans and with his bare arms, looked very boyish and sexy, his hand constantly straying to his penis. Laughing one minute, surly the next, he gave a very physical performance, using the whole room and what was in it.

ff At the first read-through, Jimmy threw his script on the floor and said, 'This is shit!'

Franklin Heller quoted by Susan Bluttman
Emmy magazine

ff James Dean stole the spotlight… in the role of a psychotic young janitor delivered a magnetic performance that brought a routine meller alive… Dean's performance was in many ways reminiscent of Marlon Brando's in *Streetcar* but he gave his role the individuality and nuances of its own which it required. He's got quite a future ahead of him.

Chan *Variety*

Walter Hampden, James Dean and Betsy Palmer in *Death Is My Neighbour*

During a seminar at The Museum of Television and Radio in New York, Heller described how Dean, despite having been warned a number of times, kept on swearing on the set and so, out of deference to Walter Hampden, an elderly and distinguished actor, he decided to fire him. Hampden intervened on Dean's behalf, saying that though Dean was untutored and untrained, he was enormously talented and that it would be wrong for them to stifle and retard his career.

Hampden was the last of the great American actor-managers and in the 1920s had played Hamlet, Macbeth, Shylock, Richard III and, most famously, Cyrano de Bergerac.

Rex Newman

Series	The Big Story
Network	NBC
Date	11 September 1953

Writer	Alvin Boretz
Director	Stuart Rosenberg
Producer	Barnard J. Procktor
Narrator	Bob Sloane

Cast

John Kerr / Wendy Drew
Carl Frank / Donald McKee
Ken Walker / Bobby Nick
Susan Harris / James Dean

The Big Story was a weekly dramatization of crimes solved by reporters. In this episode Rex Newman, reporter for *The Globe and News*, helped the authorities to uncover a trail of robbery and murder by a trio of teenagers.

Glory in the Flower

Series	Omnibus
Network	CBS
Date	4 October 1953

Writer	William Inge
Director	Andrew McCullough
Producer	Fred Rickey

Role	**Cast**
Jackie	Jessica Tandy
Howie	Hume Croyn
Bus	Ed Binns
Salesman	Frank McHugh
Joker	Mark Rydell
Bronco	James Dean

Omnibus was the most outstanding and longest running cultural series in the history of American commercial television and there were no commercials. In 1953 they produced Orson Welles's *King Lear* (directed by Peter Brook) and plays by James Thurber, Ernest Hemingway, Carson McCullers, John Steinbeck, T. S. Eliot and William Inge.

Glory in the Flower, specially written for television, was practically a solo turn for Jessica Tandy, who had created Blanche DuBois in Tennessee Williams's *A Streetcar Named Desire* on Broadway opposite Marlon Brando's Stanley Kowalski.

There was a time when Inge (1917–13), author of *Come Back Little Sheba* and *Picnic* (which had just opened and won the Pulitzer Prize) was bracketed with Williams and Arthur Miller but that time has long since passed, though he has been having a comeback in America recently.

The play was a typical Inge piece about the frustrations of small town life in the mid-West. The setting was a roadhouse, close to a jerk town, and it was the only place where the kids could hang out. The theme was established in the opening line: 'Nothing ever stays the same.'

Tandy played Jackie, a teacher, 'a silly dame', fast approaching 40, who still behaved like a schoolgirl. She had thrown herself at Bus Riley ('the best-looking guy I ever saw') when they were at high school and she had been waiting for him to come back so she could throw herself at him all over again. But Bus (Ed Binns) was no longer the sweet man she remembered but a horny, bad-natured womanizer in a spiffey suit peddling big stories about himself. Disillusioned by his attitude to her and his boorish, bullying behaviour towards the kids, she discovered she was no longer nuts about him and walked out on him, only to spoil the gesture by coming back and saying that she didn't want there to be any hard feelings between them.

Inge's subsidiary theme was about youth. 'Maybe we make it too tough for them,' said the philosophical bartender (played by Hume Croyn, Jessica Tandy's husband). 'Maybe they're afraid.'

Dean was cast as Bronco, one of a number of teenagers jitterbugging to the Bill Hayley and the Comets hit, 'Crazy Man, Crazy' on a juke box. He forced his attentions on Jackie.

'Dance with a real cat!' he cried. 'Hey, this is the atomic age, man.'

They danced a few steps and Jackie went sprawling. He was mortified. 'It wasn't my fault. After all, I didn't do it on purpose. You don't have to blame me.'

He retreated to the men's room.

'Everybody blames me!' he moaned to the door, a pretty unsympathetic listener.

Bronco, who was already in trouble with the juvenile authorities for smoking marijuana, had brought his own liquor. He was under-age and couldn't be served alcohol. (Dean never had any difficulty in looking under-age.) Soon he was rolling drunk and the bartender decided the time had come for him to leave.

'What's going to become of you?' he asked.

Bronco didn't give a damn. 'I'll manage all right, thank you. You don't have to worry about me.'

Bus decided to straighten him out and grabbed him by the lapels. 'Don't give us any back talk, you little goon. You kids litter up the place causing trouble… I know how to handle his kind.' And he slapped Bronco's face. There were gasps of horror. It was such a little slap.

'You're a phoney,' retorted Bronco. Bus knocked him down. 'No one's going to tell me what to do!' he whined, lying sprawled on the floor.

'Yes, they are, kid,' said the bartender. And Dean was carried out.

Inge's final message was that they all had to grow up; and that included Jackie.

❝ He had a terrible attitude – very snotty, very arrogant. As he started to read for me he put his feet on the table, pulled a knife from his boot and stuck it into the table.

Andrew McCullough *Emmy*

❝ It made for highclass, varied hour-and-half of entertainment, with just an occasional bit of pretentiousness or archness creeping in.

Bron *Variety*

Glory in the Flower was reworked and filmed in 1965 as *Bus Riley's Back in Town* with Michael Parks and Ann-Margret and directed by Harvey Hart.

Keep Our Honor Bright

Series	Kraft Television Theater
Network	NBC
Date	14 October 1953
Writer	George Roy Hill
Director	Maury Holland
Producer	Maury Holland

Role	Cast
Matt	Michael Higgins
Sally	Joan Potter
Mr Matthewson	Larry Fletcher
Jim	James Dean
Dean	Addison Richard
Mr Todd	Graham Denton
Mr Baldwin	Richard Bishop
Mr Wilson	Rusty Lane
Mr Stone	Calvin Thomas
Mr Langley	David White
News Commentator	George Roy Hill
Ed	Don Dubbins
Ross	John Dutra
Peter	Peter Fernandez
Tom	Cricket Skilling
Bill	Jim Hickman
News Analyst	Larry Elliott
Marillyn	Betty Gibson
Nurse	Edith Gresham
Hines	Andy Milligan
Ben	Jack Finnegan
Porter	T. J. Sydney
Students	Diane Hale,
	Joan Taylor,
	Donald Hernly,
	Bradford Dillman,
	Hal Hamilton,
	Ronald Jacoby
	Robert Stonebridge,
	Jan Musiel

The early 1950s were the years when Senator Joseph McCarthy presided over the notorious investigations of the Senate Committee of Internal Security. 'Are you or have you ever been a member of the Communist party?' asked McCarthy, who sought to extort confessions from his victims and to get them to name their associates.

The most famous play to be directly inspired by the hearings was Arthur Miller's *The Crucible*, which was first produced on the New York stage in January 1953. *Keep Our Honor Bright*, produced in the same year and also clearly influenced by the hearings, was written by George Roy Hill, who would later go on to direct such movies as *Butch Cassidy and the Sundance Kid* and *The Sting*.

The story concerned a scandal at a prominent American university. A special meeting of the Student Honor Committee was convened to confront a student who had been caught cheating during a biology examination. The student was played by James Dean.

Jim (that was the character's name) sat in a low chair. He wore a dark suit. The other students wore light suits and remained standing. Jim was deferential, soft-spoken, his head was bowed, his shoulders hunched, his eyes down, his eyebrows arched. Five feet eight inches high, 135 pounds, he was a boy among older boys, and he cowered.

Jim admitted his guilt immediately. 'I don't know why I did it. It just happened.' (He had inadvertently found the examination paper, which somebody had carelessly thrown in a bin.) 'I don't like to beg,' he said, embarrassing everybody. 'I'm begging now. Please don't expel me, please.' He was near to tears. The committee decided he must be expelled.

There was a shot of Dean in the corridor walking back into the room to hear the verdict, the corridor dwarfing him, making

him seem even smaller and more vulnerable.

'You must change your minds,' he pleaded. 'What if there were others?' In an attempt to save his own skin he was prepared to name 40 other students who had also seen the examination paper in advance.

Later, off-screen, unable to face expulsion and his folks (who had all been to the same college), Jim took an overdose of sleeping tablets, leaving a note which blew the whole incident wide open.

His suicide attempt failed. One of the students who had cheated visited him in hospital, bringing with her a toy spider which she plonked on his chest. Jim (good Joe that he was) confessed to her that he was the one who had given all the names. It had never

occurred to him that the committee would turn them all in.

As always Dean was very good at mixing the laughter and the tears, laughing at the spider and blubbing for what he had done.

'The one thing I did they said was honorable – it's the one thing I'm most ashamed of.' He turned his tortured face away from the camera.

The university was faced with a problem: to expel or not to expel the cheating students? The students who hadn't cheated issued an ultimatum. They would strike if the cheaters were not expelled. The governors were divided as to what they should do, arguing that the whole nation cheated.

Life Sentence

Series	Campbell Soundstage
Network	NBC
Date	16 October 1953
Writer	S. Lee Progostin
Adaptor	Margaret Kleckner
Director	Garry Simpson
Producer	Martin Horrell

Cast

James Dean / Georgann Johnson
Nicholas Saunders / Matt Crowley
Charles Mendick

James Dean and
Georgann Johnson in
Life Sentence

Jean Ryder (Georgann Johnson) lived in a small factory town near an open prison. A convict, Hank Bradon (James Dean), forced his attentions on her. She begged her husband (Nicholas Saunders) to take her away and when he refused she shot him. She told the police it was an accident and that she believed a prisoner was responsible. She got away with her story until Hank was freed and came to her home and tried to persuade her to go off with him.

There was a dramatic scene on her porch when they met for the first time.

Hank: Every time I see you it strikes me how out of place you are here.
Jean: This is my porch. If you don't get off my porch immediately, I'll call the guard.
Hank: If you do I'll bash your skull in.

He then went on to tell her about his masturbatory fantasy of a girl in a yellow bathing suit and how he used to dream of her 'on a surf board swimming across white fluffy waves'. He grabbed her as she made to leave.

Jean: You're hurting me.
Hank: First time I touched a woman in five years. (*The music on the soundtrack came in with a strong beat.*) Ask me what my name is. My name is Hank Bradon. Before I was a convict, I was an intern, a good intern with a bad temper. My only weakness was… never mind. Now you say to me, Hello Hank Bradon. (*He held her tighter.*)
Jean: You're hurting me.
Hank: Go on say it. (*The music got more urgent.*) Make believe I'm carrying your books home from school and you're hysterical with joy because my name is right, my money is right. I belong to a good fraternity. My car is a long yellow convertible.

It was these abrupt changes in mood which made Dean's performance so unnerving. One minute he was being all sentimental, the next he was psychotic. The deadly earnestness with which Dean spoke his last lines was chilling. Her physical danger was palpable; he was quite capable of killing and raping her.

It was a pity that the director should have allowed him to go right over the top at the end of the scene and rip open his shirt in an unnecessary and embarrassing theatrical gesture in which he seemed to be reaching out for a Marlon Brando-like climax and missing it.

The Bells of Cockaigne

Series	Armstrong's Circle Theatre
Network	NBC
Date	17 November 1953
Writer	George Lowther
Director	James Sheldon
Producer	Hudson Faussett

Role	Cast
Pat	Gene Lockhart
Joey	James Dean
Jonesy	Vaughn Taylor
Margie	Donalee Marans
Rivnock	John Dennis
Kreuger	Karl Lukas
Mike	William Thunhurst
Liddie	Si Vario
Sam	Tige Andrews

Armstrong's Circle Theatre was one of the major series of American Television's 'Golden Age'. They provided family entertainment and the dramatizations were often based on true events.

The Bells of Cockaigne may have been true but it felt like a bit of Irish blarney. 'When you get something which you've been wanting for a long time, you hear the bells of Cockaigne,' explained Pat, the janitor, played by Gene Lockhart in his best stage-Irish manner. (Cockaigne was an imaginary island of luxury and idleness.)

James Dean was cast as Joey, a young stevedore, struggling to support his wife and asthmatic son. The first shot of Dean saw him stripped to the waist, lugging boxes. He was a small skinny guy surrounded by beefy men. It was rare thing to see Dean stripped in a film and he looked so emaciated it was easy to believe that not only was Joey starving but that Jimmy Dean himself was on a poverty diet and finding it hard to make ends meet.

Joey was up to his ears in debt and unable to get any more credit at the drug store; and,

if that weren't enough, his pay was docked because he had stayed home to look after his sick child.

'Life has sure kicked that kid around,' observed one worker. 'Ever since I have known him, he's had nothing but bad luck. Made him kind of hard to get along with… He can be a sore head.' He might have been talking about Dean.

Janitor Pat, a widower, took a fatherly interest in Joey and was always giving him advice, which was not always appreciated.

'I don't want advice from you or anybody else. Sympathy don't pay no doctors' bills.'

In a desperate effort to settle those arrears, Joey decided to gamble his wages. He lost the whole paypacket.

Pat played the lucky dollar bill lottery each week, hoping to win $500, which would pay for a journey back to Ireland before he died. He wanted to see the village where he was born. Nobody was surprised when he won the lottery and nobody was surprised when the the bells of Cockaigne played on the soundtrack.

The sentimental good-luck-God-bless-you ending could now be seen coming a mile off. When the kindly janitor learned that Joey had lost all his money, he gave him his winning dollar bill, pretending Joey had just dropped it.

'You know it's the first time we ever had a lucky break,' said the young stevedore, near to tears, his voice cracking.

The bells of Cockaigne played once more. Well, it would have been a strange t'ing, to be sure, if they hadn't, now wouldn't it?

A Long Time Till Dawn

Series	Kraft Television Theater
Network	NBC
Date	11 November 1953
Writer	Rod Serling
Director	Dick Dunlap
Producer	Dick Dunlap

Role	Cast
Joe Harris	James Dean
Barbie Harris	Naomi Riordan
Fred Harris	Ted Osborn
Lieutenant Case	Robert Simon
Poppa Golden	Rudolph Weiss
Mr Gilchrist	O. Tolbert Hewitt
Tramp	Billy M. Greene
Paul	Pud Flanagan
Sully	Robert Cass

A Long Time Till Dawn offered Dean his first major television role. Joe Harris ('a 23-year-old kid with a fresh country boy's face') just released from prison, had discovered his wife had left him. He sat at a table in a delicatessen fiddling with his coffee spoon, very Method, very distracting, smoking a cigarette, and occasionally sucking the collar of his shirt. The latter bit of business so impressed Martin Landau that he remembered it 30 years later when he was being interviewed in the documentary, *Hollywood: The Rebels*.

Playwright Rod Serling described Joe as 'violence with big blue eyes' and there was no shortage of clues in the text as to how Dean should play him: 'a strange boy… he's a poet and he's a gangster… a sensitive kid but without remorse or conscience… he's got brains but his logic is like a little boy's.'

Joe had already been twice in jail, once for stealing and once for beating a man up. When he learned that it was the delicatessen owner who had told his wife to leave him, he beat him up, too, and so badly that the old man died.

One minute Joe was gentle ('if you could have seen the look on his face, you would want to take him in your arms like a little boy') and the next he was a thug. It was either love or hate. There was nothing in between. It was this threatening uncertainty which was so unsettling. A vicious streak was always ready to burst. 'Wipe his eyes with one hand, slit your throat with the other,' observed the cynical cop who'd been on the beat for 18 years and knew Joe for a hoodlum and liar. Joe didn't like him either and wiped his hand clean on the back of his trousers after the cop had shaken his hand.

Joe returned home to a leafy New Jersey suburb for the first time in three years. Dad (who had never been able to understand his son) had kept his room exactly as it had been when he was a teenager just in case he should ever come back.

'Give me chance!' he pleaded, hands outstretched. 'I'm not going to make these mistakes any more. Haven't you ever made a mistake?' he asked, anticipating Jim Stark's relationship with his father in *Rebel Without a Cause*.

One of Dean's best scenes was with his wife in his bedroom. Lying on the bed, he seized her hand and started chatting her up, all sexy, wanting to make love. (She had never understood him, either.) 'You're all against me!' he railed, all surly. 'He had no business hitting me… I didn't mean to kill him.' (She wanted him to give himself up.) 'Go on! You're just like the rest of them. You're all against me, all of you.' He grabbed a revolver from his suitcase.

'All right, Joe,' said the cynical cop who had finally caught up with him and was in the street below. 'Time to be smart. You've got three minutes, Joe. Put down your gun and come down or we'll come in after you.' The cop had obviously seen a lot of gangster movies.

James Dean in
A Long Time Till Dawn

'You're crazy, all of you, crazy,' screamed Joe, getting more and more hysterical. 'It was not supposed to be like this. I just wanted it the way it was.'

He slammed the door, clutched his baseball to his chest and curled up in a foetal position on the bed, cradling pistol and ball, very Freudian, not knowing whether to cry or laugh and doing both, very childlike, very vulnerable, very James Dean.

Joe then appeared at the window with gun and ball yelling at the top of his voice, 'Come and get me!' – very James Cagney, very 1930s Warner Bros. The police let him have it and he fell out of the window in the way actors do in films.

Ted Osborn, as the father, tended to ham up his role in a different sort of way. He was less Method, more old-fashioned Melodrama; but then his dialogue (with lines

like, 'Will we ever be able to sleep again?') was not much help.

Rod Serling was one of America's major television writers. Three years later he wrote what is probably his best-known play, *Requiem For A Heavyweight*, acted by Jack Palance in the US and by the then unknown Sean Connery on BBC Television when Palance dropped out at the last minute.

66 Jimmy Dean played the part in *A Long Time Till Dawn* brilliantly. I can't imagine anyone playing that particular role better... There was an excitement and intensity about him that he transmitted to the television audience.

Rod Serling quoted in National Film Theatre booklet

Harvest

Series	The Johnson's Wax Program
Network	NBC
Date	23 November 1953
Writer	Sandra Michael
Director	James Sheldon
Producer	Robert Montgomery

Role	Cast
Ellen Zelanka	Dorothy Gish
Carl Zelanka	Ed Begley
Gramp	Vaughn Taylor
Paul Zelanka	James Dean
Arlene	Reba Tassell
Chuck	John Connell
Joe	John Dennis
Herb	Joseph Foley
Louise	Nancy Sheridan
Fran	Mary Lou Taylor
Kip	Tommy Taylor
Mr Franklin	Frank Tweddell
Kitty	Pidge Jameson
Billy	Peter Lazer

Harvest, introduced by Robert Montgomery, was a story of farming life, a parable for Thanksgiving. The oppressive Quaker atmosphere must surely have brought back many memories for Dean of his own Quaker upbringing on his uncle and aunt's farm in Fairmount, Indiana.

The religious theme was hammered home. There was a running commentary which never stopped preaching. Hymn singing regularly punctuated the action. 'Bless the folk who dwell within,' blared the soundtrack. 'Keep them pure and free from sin.'

Mr Zelanka (Ed Begley), whose family had been farmers in the Midwest for aeons, wanted his son, Paul (James Dean), to stay on the farm. His two elder boys had already left to marry and pursue other careers. But Paul hated farming and his girl friend wanted him to go to the city.

Awkward and painfully shy, he sat at her parents' dinner table, wearing her dad's large jacket (because he had turned up without a jacket) and learned to be ashamed of his own family's table manners.

There were lots of single shots of Dean, the good-natured country boy, brooding: brooding at the window, brooding at the kitchen sink, brooding at the mail box, brooding on the porch, suffering always in silence.

Paul went to town to look for a job and called on his girl, carrying a couple of chickens his mom had insisted he take as a gift for her family. He arrived to find she had another beau, somebody of her own class, snottier, richer and chinless. He decided to join the navy.

The only question which then remained was whether the whole family would come home for dinner on Thanksgiving Day? The question was barely asked before they were all there sitting round the table (Dean looked very cute in his sailor suit) and one of the elder sons was saying he was coming back to work on the farm. The only person who didn't turn up was grandpa. He, unfortunately, hadn't been able to make it, having died just days before his 100th birthday. But, never mind, they kept him a place at table anyway.

Harvest ended with more rousing hymn singing.

The Little Woman

Series   Danger
Network   CBS
Date   30 March 1954

Writer   Joe Scully
Director   Andrew McCullough
Producer   Andrew McCullough

Cast
Lydia Reed / Lee Bergere
James Dean

66 One of the most generous performances I've ever seen. Not an ounce of ego in it.

Andrew McCullough

Augie (James Dean), a young delinquent, had got himself involved as transmission belt for a couple of travelling burglars and safe-breakers, who were intending to steal plates used for counterfeiting. On the run from the police, he was provided with shelter by an eight-year-old girl (Lydia Reed) in her playhouse in a slum alley. Apart from the local cop (Lee Bergere), Augie was her only friend.

Joe Scully, a leading television writer, wrote the role specially for Dean.

66 It wasn't much of a yarn but the thesping was good, particularly that of Lydia and the characteristics of each player were skilfully developed.

Trau *Variety*

Run Like a Thief

Series   Philco TV Playhouse
Network   NBC
Date   5 September 1954

Writer   Sam Hall
Director   Jeffrey Hayden
Producer   Gordon Duff

Cast
Kurt Kasznar / Gusti Huber
James Dean / Barbara O'Neil

A waiter (Kurt Kasznar), working in a hotel, found a diamond bracelet which belonged to the proprietress (Barbara O'Neill). He decided to keep it and gave it to his wife (Gusti Huber), an action totally out of keeping with his character. His young protégé (James Dean) was completely disillusioned when he found out what he had done.

66 James Dean, as the boy, Kasznar's protégé, emerged as a rather unclear figure even though his thesping was beyond reproach. He was the man the script forgot to explain and the void made a difference.

Hift *Variety*

Padlock

Series   Danger
Network   CBS
Date   9 November, 1954

Writer   Louis Peterson
Drector   John Frankenheimer
Producer   n/a

Cast
James Dean / Mildred Dunnock
Dorothy Stickney / David Hardison / Ken Konophia

Padlock was a suspense story. Dean was cast as a gunman fleeing from the police and robbing an eccentric old lady (Mildred Dunnock).

James Dean and
Mildred Dunnock in
Padlock

I'm a Fool

Series	General Electric Theater
Network	CBS
Date	14 November 1954

Writer	Sherwood Anderson
Adaptor	Arnold Schulman
Director	Don Medford
Producer	Mort Abrahams

Role	Cast
Narrator	Eddie Albert
The Boy	James Dean
Lucy	Natalie Wood
Burt	Roy Glenn
Mother	Eve March
Wilbur	Leon Taylor
Elinor	Gloria Costillo
Mildred	Fiona Hall

General Electric Theater provided television with a long-running dramatic anthology of wide-ranging material. *I'm a Fool* was an adaptation of a classic short story by Sherwood Anderson, a minor yet seminal figure in American literature, whose simple and direct style influenced many authors, including Ernest Hemingway.

A revival of the production, shortly after Dean's death, was introduced by Ronald Reagan and described by him as one of the landmarks in Dean's career. 'Those of us,' said the future President, 'who worked with Jimmy Dean carry an image of his intense struggle for a goal beyond himself and curiously enough that's the story of the boy he plays tonight.'

The story, set at the turn of the century in the days of the buggy and horse, was narrated by Eddie Albert and acted by Dean who played Albert's younger self, a simple, innocent, 19-year-old country lad, who left home to become a swipe (a stable boy) at a race track.

'Remember one thing,' said his ma as he set off, 'clothes make the man. Put up a good front and the world is yours.'

He fell in love with Lucy, a beautiful, elegant, rich city girl and then did 'the biggest dumb fool thing' in his life. ('Even when I think about it now I want cry and kick myself.') He bought himself a new brown derby hat, went to a hotel, where all the dudes hung out with their Windsor ties and canes, and passed himself off as a swell. He claimed to be the owner of a big house and stable and assumed the name and address of the local bigbug, Walter Mathers from Mariettah, Ohio. Amazingly, Lucy and her two toffy-nosed friends fell for his deception.

Amazingly, because he didn't look like a swell. In his derby hat, his standup collar, he looked and sounded what he was: a likeable, naive country boy, a dreamer, a boob smoking a big fat 25 cent cigar, making it up as he went along. His fabrication would lose him the love of his life.

Dean and Natalie Wood (cast as Lucy) played their last scene beautifully. 'I know what you want to tell me,' she said. 'You do?' he replied, all surprised. She thought he wanted to tell her he loved her when he wanted to tell her who he really was but he never got round to it before she boarded the train back to Ohio because she was chattering away and he couldn't get a word in edgeways.

'I don't know your name. I don't know where to write.'

'It's all right,' she replied, as the train was moving off, 'I know where to write.'

'But Lucy,' he muttered as the train disappeared into the darkness, 'I'm not Walter...' And Dean, true to Sherwood's text, 'busted out and cried like a kid.' His frustration and anguish were both sad and comic.

Don Medford's charming production was highly artificial in its staging, lighting, back projection and sound effects. The tale was acted and mimed as if it were an

impressionistic play by either Thornton Wilder or William Saroyan. The sets, horses and the crowds at the races were all cutouts and the actors, very stylized, were often seen in silhouette.

Eddie Albert, first-rate as the narrator, spoke directly to the cameras, reliving the romantic longings and agonies of his youth. He was the perfect actor for Anderson's gee-whizz vernacular.

66 He was not difficult to work with, but he could be frustrating. I would just stage him and let him go. Most live shows had three cameras; however, I always had a fourth camera on Jimmy and followed him wherever he went. It was worth it.

Don Medford

66 Most of us... were acting as if we were on a stage. Jimmy brought a whole different 'inside' thing that was like the Actors Studio, but with a sense of humour in it, too.

Eddie Albert

66 The set and process work (which didn't always work properly) had a tendency to weaken the sincerity of Don Medford's direction and some excellent thespic work, particularly Dean... a sensitive and moving performance.

Kap *Daily Variety*

66 ... a brooding powerful young actor with a definite career before him.

Hollywood Reporter

The Dark, Dark Hour

Listed in TV Guide as **Out of the Night**
Series   General Electric Theater
Network   CBS
Date   12 December 1954

Writer   Arthur Steuer
Director   Don Medford
Producer   Mort Abrahams

Cast

Ronald Reagan / James Dean
Constance Ford / Jack Simmons

*James Dean and
Ronald Reagan in
The Dark, Dark Hour*

A small-town doctor (Ronald Reagan) and his
wife (Constance Ford) were held prisoner in
their home by a juvenile delinquent (James
Dean), who armed with a pistol, forced him to
perform an illegal operation on his wounded
friend (Jack Simmons). The doctor finally
overpowered him in an unconvincing climax.
There were two contradictory reports about
the production in *Daily Variety*.

" We heard many good words for James
Dean's performance on Sunday G. E. Theater,
with high praise for the gangster lingo.

Television columnist *Daily Variety*

" Reagan's part is negatively enacted and
Constance Ford as his wife is called upon for
illogical action as she fails to understand why
her husband, though covered by a gun, doesn't
immediately attack the delinquent. This role is
played by James Dean, but he has been called
upon to overact.

Whit *Daily Variety*

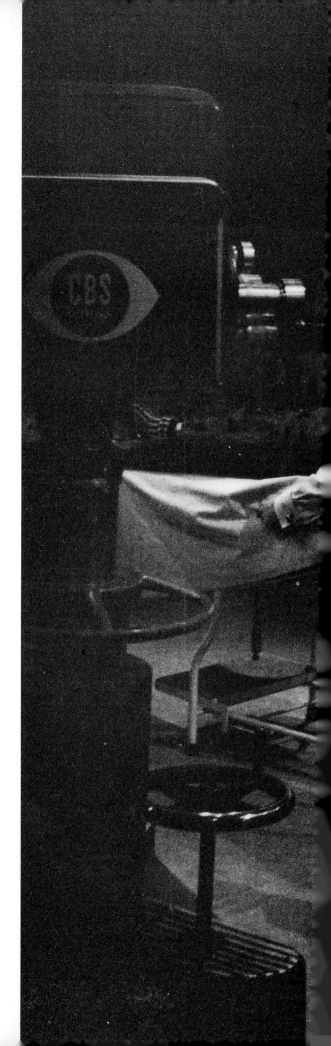

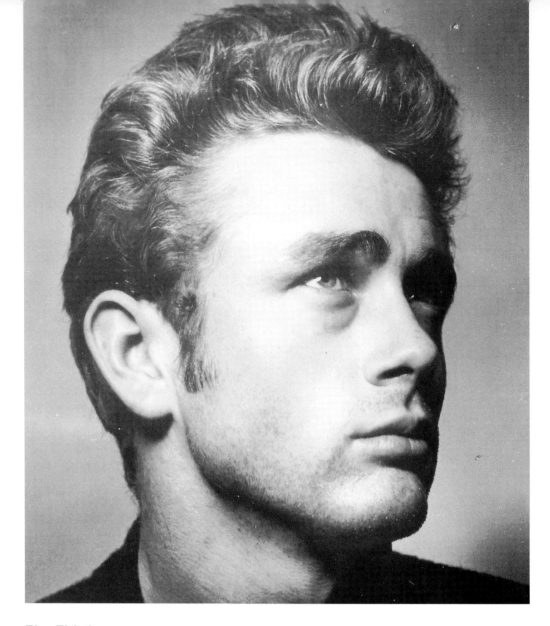

The Thief

Series	The United States Steel Hour
Network	ABC
Date	4 January 1955
Writer	Henri Bernstein
Adaptor	Arthur Arent
Director	Vincent J. Donehue
Producer	John Haggott

Role	Cast
Marie-Louise Voyson	Diana Lynn
Charles Lagarde	Paul Lukas
Isabelle Lagarde	Mary Astor
Phillipe Voyson	Patric Knowles
Fernand Lagarde	James Dean
D'Arnault Olivier	Nehemian Persoff
Michel	Jerry Morris

French dramatist Henri Bernstein dominated the Paris stage between 1900 and 1907, shocking and delighting audiences with his portraits of a grasping, materialistic society.

The Thief, first performed in 1906, was a scandalous success and the following year it was seen in London with George Alexander and Irene Vanbrugh, and in New York with Kyrle Bellow and Margaret Illington. Its manifest artificiality was criticized on both sides of the Atlantic.

Production values were high. The sets were richly furnished. Dean made his entrance down a curving staircase, wearing a smoking jacket. He was cast as Fernand Lagarde, the gentle, polite, softly spoken, well-mannered, sad-eyed younger son of an aristocratic family. His eyebrows were arched and his hair was beautifully coiffured. Fernand, upset that his father had remarried, was not very sociable.

On a terrace overburdened with shrubbery, he flirted with a childhood sweetheart, the not-very-bright Marie-Louise, who had just returned his love letters. She was 20 and a married woman. He was only 19 and very sweet and very intense in his schoolboy way.

'Don't talk to me as though I were a child,' he said, speaking like a child. 'When I'm not seeing you I feel shut off in the world.'

Meanwhile, there was a detective in the house, pretending to be a house-guest. He was there at the invitation of Lagarde père. Over 12,000 French francs had disappeared from his wife's room and he was anxious to know who had stolen them. The detective was convinced that the culprit was his 'unfortunate son'. The boy, who had only a small allowance, was seeing an actress with expensive tastes and had just lost a lot of money at the races.

'There's nothing unfortunate about his character,' said Lagarde , bristling. 'He's shy, he's poetic and he's introspective. Since when is that unfortunate in a Frenchman at 19?'

To everybody's surprise, Fernand admitted he had stolen the money. But why had he done it? The answer – not too difficult to guess – was he had stolen it for Marie-Louise's sake. She needed the cash to buy pretty clothes to satisfy (so she said) the pride and sensuality of her husband and she had asked him to steal it and he, being in love with her, had done it.

'How long has this calf-love capable of deep feeling being going on?' asked the husband, convinced she had been having affair with the boy. It was the script's only witty line.

The truth had come out in a bedroom scene, one of those melodramatic exchanges between husband and wife so popular with the Edwardian theatregoer. The husband had immediately blamed himself *and asked his wife to forgive him*!

'We men make one mistake. We make the women we love think pleasing us is the only reason. It's our fault. We have no excuse.' (It probably sounded better in French.) Their reconciliation was totally unconvincing.

Lagarde decided that it would be best to send his son to the plantations in Brazil for two years. (Wayward sons in Edwardian plays were invariably sent abroad for two years.)

'You mustn't do anything foolish,' said Marie-Louise, a bit rich coming from her.

'Do you know what my love for you is like?' he replied. 'Do you know, do you? Don't be afraid. I'll be all right, I promise you.' And he burst into tears. It would have been more surprising if he hadn't.

The Thief may have been mechanical, romantic rubbish, but Dean acted his role of 'hero and young imp' with total sincerity within the conventions of the genre and, contrary to what Mary Astor said, he was totally articulate.

❝ I found out how hard it was to work with a mumbler when I was acting with the late Jimmy Dean in a live TV show before his great success. Jimmy was six feet away from me in one scene and I could barely hear what he was saying and what I could hear seemed to have very little to do with the script.

Mary Astor *A Life in Film*

❝ … maladroitly attempting to combine the boyish with the Charles Boyerish.

Gilbert Adair *Independent*

The Unlighted Road

Series	Schiltz Playhouse of Stars
Network	CBS
Date	6 May 1955
Writer	Walter C. Brown
Director	Justus Addiss
Producer	William Self

Role	Cast
Jeff Latham	James Dean
Mike Deegan	Murvyn Vye
Matt Schrieber	Edgar Stehli
Ann Burnett	Pat Hardy
Captain	Voltaire Perkins
Roy Montana	Charles Wagenheim

James Dean and
Pat Hardy in
The Unlighted Road

The Unlighted Road, a half-hour thriller, was Dean's last television film, made just before *East of Eden* was released. He was cast as Jeff Latham, a Korean War veteran, recently discharged, a long way from home and drifting around, doing odd jobs.

Dean, wearing a leather jacket and smoking the inevitable cigarette, wandered into a dirty, roadside diner, looking like a younger version of Marlon Brando in *The Wild One*.

Jett was in search of a steady job and a steady girl. The owner of the diner offered him a job after he had mended his dirty tea urn. A steady girl turned up almost immediately.

Hard-working and decent, Jeff didn't want to get mixed up in anything crooked. However, unbeknown to him, his boss was dealing in stolen goods. He was driving along a dark road at night delivering a package when he looked in his mirror and realized he was being shot at by a cop in a pursuing car. The cop smacked into a tree and was killed.

The man for whom the diner's owner was working then attempted a bit of blackmail in

order to make Jeff continue working for them. He threatened to report the crash to the police. 'You know what happens to cop-killers,' he said. 'They burn.'

Jeff, having nobody else to turn to, went to his new girl friend ('I'm in big trouble, big trouble, I've got to give myself up') but then refused to let her involve either herself or her father.

As it turned out it was a good thing he did give himself up, otherwise he might have spent the rest of his life sweating for a murder he hadn't committed. The cop wasn't a cop. He was another crook and he hadn't died in the crash, either. He was shot by the bad guys and shoved into the lake, car and all, and left to drown.

It was a pretty poor script. There was no suspense and no characterization, only a few good close-ups of Dean's face. Still, such was the demand for anything with him in it, that *The Unlighted Road* was shown no less than five times after his death.

❝ Dean projects an interesting, off-beat personality, but underplays so much his performance loses some of its effectiveness.

Daku *Daily Variety*

Highway Safety Commercial

Date   Taped 17 September 1955

The commercial was made by the National Safety Council a few weeks before James Dean died. He had come over from the set of *Giant* to be interviewed by actor Gig Young. He sat there slumped in a chair, still in costume, his shirt open, a stetson perched on his head, smoking, and playing with a rope. Sloppy and shy, he looked just like a kid, who had never appeared in front of a camera before and couldn't wait for it to be all over. Young in his suit and tie, looked as well-groomed and as wooden as a shop window's dummy. The two men sat side by side, poles apart.

The commercial began with Dean mumbling away modestly about his recent race track wins at Palm Springs before he got down to the nitty-gritty. He admitted he used to fly around quite a bit and had taken a lot of

unnecessary chances in the past, but since he had started racing he 'was extra cautious because no one knows what they're doing half the time… I don't have the urge to speed on the highway.'

'Do you have any special advice for young people who drive?' asked Young as Dean was walking out of the door.

'Take it easy driving. The life you might save might be mine.'

The commercial has an amateurish quality and its sole interest now is its terrible double irony: one, that Dean, a notoriously reckless driver, should have made the commercial in the first place; and two, that he should have died only 13 days after he had made it.

Gig Young and James Dean in highway safety commercial

Opposite: James Dean in *Rebel Without a Cause*

film

Sailor Beware!

Director	Hal Walker
Studio	Paramount
Release	January 1951
Producer	Hal Wallis
Screenplay	Martin Rackin and
	James Allardice
Play by	Kenyon Nicholson and
	Charles Robinson
Adaptor	Elwood Ullman
Additional dialogue	John Grant
Photography	Daniel L. Fapp
Songs	Mack David, Jerry Livingston,
	Thurston Knudson

Role	Cast
Al Crowthers	Dean Martin
Melvin Jones	Jerry Lewis
Corinne Calvet	Corinne Calvet
Hilda Jones	Marion Marshall
Lardoski	Robert Strauss
Blayden	Vince Edwards
Commander Lane	Lief Erickson
Guest appearance	Betty Hutton

Sailor Beware! was a remake of the 1942 Dorothy Lamour–William Holden musical, *The Fleet's In*. The comedy was strictly for Dean Martin and Jerry Lewis fans with Lewis up to his usual frenetic, moronic, cross-eyed, crybaby antics. The sailors took on bets whether Lewis would be able to kiss real-life singer Corinne Calvet.

The British and American critics failed to understand how the two actors had become the second most popular box office attraction in the United States and advised their readers to give the film a wide berth. One reviewer thought they were the unfunniest couple since Burke and Hare.

There were nevertheless two amusing scenes. The first, in a locker room, was a straight bit of vaudeville patter with Martin playing stooge to Lewis who was pretending to be a punch-drunk, cauliflower-brained professional boxer in order to frighten off his amateur opponent. The scene in the ring was one of the funniest fights since Charlie Chaplin's silent short, *The Champ*. Lewis ran round the perimeter as if he were on a racing track, and then danced about, showing off some nifty footwork while landing silly harmless punches.

James Dean was cast as Lewis's opponent's second. He tied on the boxer's gloves, did a bit of unconvincing shoulder massage, and eavesdropped on the patter. He had one line of dialogue ('That guy's a professional') and contrary to report, the line has not been cut. For the rest, it was just a matter of climbing in and out of the ring and observing Lewis's clowning.

Fixed Bayonets!

Director	Samuel Fuller
Studio	20th Century-Fox
Release	November 1951
Producer	Jules Buck
Screenplay	Samuel Fuller
Novel by	John Brophy
Photography	Lucien Ballard
Music	Roy Webb

Role	Cast
Corporal Denno	Richard Basehart
Sergeant Rock	Gene Evans
Sergeant Lonergan	Michael O'Shea
Wheeler	Richard Hylton
Lieutenant Gibbs	Craig Hill
Whitey	Skip Homeier
Vogl	Henry Kulky
Walowicz	Richard Monohan
Ramirez	Paul Richards
Borcellino	Don Orlando
Paddy	Patrick Fitzgibbon
Medic	Neyle Morrow
Griff	George Wesley
Bulchek	Mel Pogue
Zablocki	George Conrad
Bigmouth	David Wolfson
Husky Doggie	Buddy Thorpe
Lean Doggie	Al Negbo
Fitz	Wyott Ordung
Jonesy	Pat Hogan

James Dean in
Fixed Bayonets!

Fixed Bayonets! was set during the Korean War in the winter of 1951. Cult director Samuel Fuller's studio-bound production concentrated on the mental stress and physical hardships that the American soldiers had to face in the snow during a rearguard action to fool the enemy that the battalion hadn't withdrawn.

The leading role was taken by Richard Basehart, cast as a sensitive corporal, who didn't want to have the responsibility of the men's lives. 'I can take an order,' he confessed. 'I can't give one.' When the three men senior to him were killed, he was forced to overcome his fear, accept command, and kill the enemy in cold blood.

Dean appeared right at the very end as a sentry with the battalion. He was seen running up. 'Lieutenant,' he said, squatting beside him, 'I think I hear them coming. Could it be the rearguard, huh?' He cocked his rifle. The line is always reported as having been cut. It hasn't been; it's in the film.

He was on the screen for about a minute at the most. Helmeted, his face blackened, and the sequence shot at night, it would have been very difficult for the most devoted fan, let alone the enemy, to recognize him.

Fixed Bayonets! was dedicated to the United States Infantry. 'As a tribute to our men', wrote Bosley Crowther in *The New York Times*, 'it is something less than inspired.'

71

Has Anybody Seen My Gal

Director	Douglas Sirk
Studio	Universal
Release	July 1952
Producer	Ted Richmond
Screenplay	Joseph Hoffman
Story	Eleanor H. Porter
Photography	Clifford Stine
Music	Joseph Gershenson

Role	Cast
Samuel Fulton	Charles Coburn
Millicent Blaisdell	Piper Laurie
Roberta Blaisdell	Gigi Perreau
Dan Stebbins	Rock Hudson
Harriet Blaisdell	Lynn Bari
Charles Blaisdell	Larry Gates
Edward Norton	Frank Ferguson
Carl Pennock	Skip Homeler
Clarissa Pennock	Natalie Schafer
Judge Wilkins	Paul Harvey
Quinn	Forrest Lewis

James Dean on the set of
Has Anybody Seen My Gal

Has Anybody Seen My Gal (with no question mark) was a lightweight comedy set in the late 1920s and punctuated with songs of the period.

A multi-millionaire (Charles Coburn), a sweet old eccentric, decided to leave his estate to the family of a woman, who had recently died, and whom he had once loved. Disguising himself as a poor man, he boarded with them, gave them an anonymous gift of $100,000, and then hung around to see how they would react to their new wealth.

The mother (Lynn Bari) bought a big house and insisted her daughter (Piper Laurie) broke off her engagement to her nice fiancé (Rock Hudson). She wanted to marry into the most important family in town. Then came the Wall Street Crash and they lost all they had. The moral was spelled out: 'It's not money that makes a person happy. It's what you do with what you have.'

Meanwhile the millionaire had taken on a job as a soda jerk in the ice-cream parlour of the family's drugstore. Dean was cast as a customer, a very laid-back college boy ordering an ice-cream sundae:

Dean: Hey, gramps, I'll have a choc malt, heavy on the choc, plenty of milk, four spoons of malt, two scoops of vanilla ice cream, one mixed with the rest, and one floating.

Coburn: Would you like to come in on Wednesday for a fitting?

It was obvious that the young man thought he was the cat's meow. Dean sat there in his chequered 1920s pullover and his little red bow-tie, his arm resting on the counter, leaning slightly back, showing off his elegant fingers. He spoke at speed and with the authority of one who was an expert on sundaes and had been ordering them for years.

Dean was on the screen for less than ten seconds. The fleeting glimpse ended with him casually dropping his floppy fedora on his head at a jaunty and sexy angle.

The film and Coburn's performance were surprisingly well-received, though Howard Thompson in *The New York Times* did have reservations: 'Mr Coburn's roguish anticipation of their confused plight and subsequent bankruptcy is a mite sadistic for a whim.'

James Dean in
Has Anybody Seen My Gal

East of Eden

Director	Elia Kazan*
Studio	Warner Bros
Date	1955
Producer	Elia Kazan
Screenplay	Paul Osborn
Photography	Ted McCord
Art Directors	James Basevi* and Malcolm Bert*
Film Editor	Owen Marks
Music	Leonard Rosenman
Set Director	George James Hopkins*

Role	Cast
Abra	Julie Harris
Cal Trask	James Dean*
Adam Trask	Raymond Massey
Sam	Burl Ives
Aron Trask	Richard Davalos
Kate	Jo Van Fleet*
Will	Albert Dekker
Ann	Lois Smith
Mr Albrecht	Harold Gordon
Joe	Timothy Carey
Piscora	Mario Siletti
Roy	Lony Chapman
Rantani	Nick Dennis

James Dean and Timothy Carey in *East of Eden*

❝ And Cain went out from the presence of the Lord, and dwelt in the land of Nod, on the east of Eden.

Genesis Chapter 4

❝ The greatest terror a child can have is that he is not loved, and rejection is the hell he fears. I think everyone in the world to a large or small extent has felt rejection. And with rejection comes anger, and with anger some kind of crime in revenge for the rejection, and with the crime guilt – and there is the story of mankind. I think if the rejection could be amputated, the human would not be what he is.

John Steinbeck *East of Eden*

Richard Davalos,
James Dean and
Julie Harris in
East of Eden

East of Eden, a 50-year saga covering the lives of two families, first published in 1952, was John Steinbeck's most ambitious novel since *The Grapes of Wrath*. Elia Kazan's film, handsomely mounted, artfully composed, concentrated on one family and limited itself to the last third of the novel. Playwright Paul Osborn's screenplay was literate and visually imaginative. The best scenes were often his and not Steinbeck's.

The action began in Monterey in 1917 just outside the city centre. A respectable, sombre-looking woman, veiled and dressed all in black, went to the bank to deposit some cash. 'You're sure in the right business,' said the teller with a smirk, the smirk leaving no doubt as to what her business was.

Cal Trask (James Dean) sat on the curb of the main street, studying his hands. He wore an open-necked, lightly coloured pullover, white trousers, and a watch dangled from his waist. He was just a kid, a sad-eyed pretty boy with almond-brown hair. He followed the woman back to the red light district and threw a stone at her house. She sent her bouncer (Timothy Carey) to deal with him.

'Would she talk to me? I just want to talk to her... You tell her I hate her.' Small, slight, vulnerable, Dean looked like a lost puppy dog.

The visit having proved abortive, he rode home on the roof of a goods train, hugging himself to keep out the cold, an image of loneliness and misery, asking (as Dean so often did) for the audience's sympathy. Cal knew he should have gone right in there and talked to her. The woman was his mother, Kate, who had shot and wounded his father when he and his twin brother, Aron, were babies and then deserted them.

Cal's father, Adam Trask (Raymond Massey, austere and severe), was a lettuce farmer, a God-fearing man, an Old Testament father, so upright, so puritanical, he had succeed in making both his sons unfit for Paradise. Deeply conservative, self-righteous and narrow-minded, he opened his mouth only to admonish and forgive. He persistently rejected Cal. He didn't understand him; he never had. The antagonism between them and his preference for Aron (Richard Davalos) was instantly established. When Cal suggested that there was a huge profit to be made out of beans, now that war was coming, Adam snubbed him. 'I'm not particularly interested in making a profit,' he said.

Abra (Julie Harris), Aron's girlfriend, described Cal as a prowler, who was always alone and didn't like anybody. She found him scary, like an animal. The scarey side was rarely visible in the film. 'I love him,' said Aron, bemused by his brother's crazy antics. The expected Cain-and-Abel tensions were absent and a long-time coming.

In the sense that Cal craved warmth and affection and that he wanted to be loved as Aron was loved, in the sense that he lived and walked alone, in the sense that he felt rejected, Dean was Steinbeck's Cal. But Steinbeck's Cal was also precociously mature and clever and this side of his character was ignored; as for the thick-skinned young man who was 'devoted to easy women, easy money' and 'wallowed in filth', this was barely hinted at.

In the ice-house, which his father had just bought, crouching between huge dripping blocks of ice which filled the CinemaScope screen, Cal spied on Aron and Abra, his eyes, baleful, red-rimmed and squinting. Then in his resentment against his father, in his jealousy of his brother, in sheer frustration, he hurled the ice down the chute.

'You're bad through and through,' said Adam.

'You're right I am bad. I've known it a long time. Aron is the good one.' (Aron was diligent, sober, upright, hard-working, and he worshipped his dead mother.)

In the Bible-reading, which followed, the room was lit and photographed initially as if it were a stage set framed by a proscenium arch, ready for the curtain to go up on a nineteenth-century drama. Slouched in his chair, head bowed, Cal was a recalcitrant child, deliberately mumbling and reading out the verse numbers when he had just been told not to do so, and then rudely pushing the Bible from him. The uneasiness of the relationship between son and father was increased by the lighting and the tilting camera angles.

In this scene Dean was also able to draw not only on the tensions which existed between him and his real father but also on the off-set tensions which existed between him and Massey, which Kazan deliberately aggravated by getting Dean to mutter obscenities which he knew would outrage Massey.

Once Aron had left the room, Cal asked why his father had never told them about their mother.

'I thought it would save you pain,' said Adam.

'Pain!' replied Cal. And Dean, his brows characteristically knit, invested the very word itself with pain. 'Talk to me, father, I've got to know who I am. I've got to know what I'm like.'

Beset with doubts about his character, he was convinced that he had inherited his evil side from his mother. Adam, who hadn't heard from Kate in years, thought she was living somewhere in the East.

'You won't tell Aron that she didn't die.'

'No, mustn't do anything to hurt Aron.' The ironic inflection was just right.

Cal revisited his mother. The trailer for the film had promised 'the wickedest woman you've ever seen'. The publicity boys had obviously read the book. Steinbeck's Kate ran the most vicious and depraved whorehouse and had the power to blackmail the whole community with her collection of damning photographs.

Kate's bitterness, arrogance, and her authority were all there in Jo Van Fleet's Oscar-winning performance; but the role was no longer the novel's monster, the woman who

James Dean in
East of Eden

had acquired her premises by murdering the owner. Under the censorship codes of the time, there could be no overt suggestion that she ran a brothel; though this did not seem to worry Kazan who invested the bar with a brothel-like atmosphere.

Cal knelt at his sleeping mother's feet, a penitent child. Minutes earlier, he had chatted up a waitress (the excellent Lois Smith) with practised sexual ease to find where her office was. Kate woke to find him staring up at her.

'Let me talk to you, please,' he begged.

She yelled for her bouncer and he was dragged along the floor and out into the long dark corridor clinging to the door, walls, anything he could get hold of.

'I want to talk to you. Talk to me, please!' The melodrama was played up to the hilt.

'She ain't no good', he told the sheriff sometime later. 'I'm no good. I knew there

Jo Van Fleet and James Dean in *East of Eden*

was a reason why I wasn't… I hate her and I hate him, too.'

The sheriff (Burl Ives, a big, burly presence), a long-time friend of his father, defended Adam saying he had more kindness, more conscience than any man he'd known and advised Cal not to sell him short. Dean, always ready to use the set, the furniture and the props around him, hugged the heater.

The scene with Abra in the field was one of the high spots of the film. The rapport between Dean and Harris was a joy to watch. Here were two Method actors, two intuitive, internal actors, totally confident in each other's acting, playfully playing off each other and improvising.

Abra identified with Cal. Her own relationship with her father had been ruined when he remarried; and because she thought she was not loved, she had thrown her stepmother's ring (worth $3,000) into the river. 'I understand kids better than grown-ups,' she said. Harris, with her freckled, solemn beauty, acted with such sensitivity and Dean listened so well, smiling and laughing. The smile and laughter were so unexpected; he was a real charmer.

Cal, in the locker room of the local gymnasium, talked to a potential backer for his bean project. (His small body barely appeared above the locker.) Cal didn't want

Aron to be involved. The sudden sharpness in Dean's voice made that absolutely clear, revealing for the first time just how deep-rooted his bitterness against his brother was. Cal wanted to go into business so that he would be able to make and give back all the money Adam had lost when he had tried to transport frozen vegetables by train. But first he needed $5,000 to get started.

He turned to the only person he knew who would have that sort of money. They walked along the road side by side. Kate asked after his brother. 'He's good,' he replied. 'I'm more like you.' She warmed to him, fully aware of the irony that her 'dirty money' was going to be used to save the 'purity' of her ex-husband. Occasionally, there were flashes of the character in the novel: 'He wanted to tie me down. Nobody holds me. Nobody tells me what to do.'

Kate did the talking. Cal, bashful, dutiful, did the listening. Dean acted with appealing awkwardness, laughing when they shared a joke about his father 'living in the Bible', giggling at the thought of blackmailing her. She quickly disabused him of that idea. He watched her keenly as she signed the cheque, his fingers itching to get hold of the cash.

'You're a likeable kid,' she said. And that was the quality Dean brought to the film. As always he looked so young, so small, so

Julie Harris and
James Dean in
East of Eden

defenceless, his face every so often (and
characteristically) turned away from the
camera. It was the things which were not said
which were so effective. But the moment Cal
tried to reach out to her, son to mother, she
would have none of it: 'GET OUT!' Jo Van
Fleet was excellent, though the tilting camera
angles were not to everybody's taste.

Not long after, there was a memorable shot
of Cal lying on his stomach in the middle of a
row of beans in a huge field, watching them
sprout, urging them to grow more quickly. He
ran up and down the lines, almost dancing,
and Leonard Rosenman's music accompanied
him with a balletic-like tinkle. (*L'Après-midi
d'un faune* – qui s'appelle Jimmy Dean?)

At the fair Abra and Cal were like a couple
of kids enjoying the distorting mirrors and
shooting range. On the Ferris wheel, groping
for truth and understanding, she confided that
Aron was such a good boy, so passionately
pure, so celibate, she felt she could never be
good enough for him. Aron wanted her to be
like his mother, a wonderful mother, the
perfect wife in a perfect marriage. Dean
caught Cal's acute embarrassment when she
tried to question him about his sex life.

The declaration of World War I led to flag-
waving jingoism and an ugly scene in which a
bewildered German storekeeper was attacked.
Aron, a pacifist, leapt to the old man's
defence. There was a flair up, fists were drawn
and Cal, going to his brother's rescue, ended
up fighting Aron.

'I tried to help him,' he confessed later to
Abra. 'Who am I kidding? I tried to kill him.
Why did I hit him so hard?' The question was
rhetorical. But just in case there were any
cinemagoers out there who didn't know the
answer, Rosenman gently reprised the love
theme, which had been heard for the first time
on the Ferris wheel when Cal and Abra had
been on the point of kissing.

Julie Harris and
James Dean in
East of Eden

Late at night, on the roof outside Abra's bedroom, he told her he'd made all the money his father had lost and asked her to help him prepare the birthday celebrations next day. The party is the most memorable scene in the film. Cal in his excitement was like a child. Adam was delighted with all the trimmings, the Chinese lanterns and bunting.

There was a close-up of Aron's bitter, malicious face glowering. The closer Cal had got to his father the more Aron had come to hate him. Their roles were reversed. In the same way that Cal had always wanted to be one up on Aron, so now Aron wanted to be one up on Cal. He played his best card, a spoiling action.

Just as his father was about to open Cal's present, he announced his engagement to

Abra, catching even her unawares.

'I can't have wished for anything nicer than this,' said Adam.

Cal watched as his father opened the packet, his eyes flicking back and forth from his father's face to the wrapped gift.

'I made it for you, all the money you lost in the lettuce business.'

'Cal,' said Adam, 'you'll have to give it back.'

'I made it for you. I want you to have it.'

Adam accused Cal of making a profit out of the war dead. 'Do you think I could take a profit from that. I don't want the money. I couldn't take the money… I'll never take it… If you want to give me a present, give me a good life, that's something I could value.'

The rejection was terrible. Cal, weeping

profusely, the body crumpled, hugged his father in his arms, and as he hugged him, the money poured over Adam's shoulders like a mini-falls.

Adam recoiled in embarrassment. 'Cal! Cal! Cal!' The rawness of the emotion took Massey (let alone Adam) completely by surprise, yet it was rooted in the novel. Much earlier in the story Steinbeck had written that Cal 'wanted to throw his arms about his father, to hug him and to be hugged by him. He wanted some wild demonstration of sympathy and love.' The scene remains to this day one of the most heartbreaking scenes in cinema.

Inarticulate with grief, Cal let out a great cry of pain ('I HATE YOU!') and then, bumping into the table, he stumbled out of the French windows and into the night. Dean always bumped into the furniture on his emotional exits.

In the garden under the willow tree, which completely enveloped them, Abra desperately tried to console the inconsolable Cal, her action angering Aron.

'Don't you ever touch her again,' he said to his brother. 'I don't trust you, you're mean and vicious and wild and you know it. Father and I have put up with every mean and vicious thing you could think of since you were a child and we've always forgiven you.'

Cal's viciousness and meanness would now be seen for the first time. In his anguish and anger he took a terrible revenge. 'Mother didn't die and go to heaven after all', he told his brother and dragged him off to the brothel and down the long, dark corridor which led to his mother's office.

'Mother,' he said, opening the door, 'Here is your other son, Aron. Aron is everything that is good, mother. Aron, say hello to your mother.'

Aron recoiled with revulsion ('No! No! No!') but Cal shoved him back into the room, throwing him on top of Kate. Kazan revelled in the melodramatic theatricality.

Cal came home to swing on the garden swing in bitter triumph. 'I know why you didn't like me,' he accused his father, 'because I'm like my mother and you never forgave yourself for having loved her.'

Asked where his brother was, he gave the inevitable reply that he was not his brother's keeper. 'I've been jealous all my life... I even tried to buy your love. But now I don't want it any more. I can't use it any more. I don't want any kind of love any more. It doesn't pay off.' Once again the tension was underlined by the distorted camera angles.

There were many who found Kazan's staging far too mannered and distracting, over-busy, overblown and over-obtrusive, full of technical virtuosity for its own sake. But, unlike many film directors of the period, he did know how to use and adapt the CinemaScope screen to his advantage.

Meanwhile, bitterly disillusioned, Aron (in a drunken stupor) had gone crazy and boarded a troop train to enlist. His father arrived too late at the station to stop him, though just in time to witness his son putting his head through the carriage window, shattering the glass, and laughing hysterically. The implication was clear, even if the audience hadn't read the novel. Aron would die in France; his brother had as good as murdered him. Richard Davalos, though never allowed to be the smug little prig of the novel, was impressive, his performance very unfairly yet inevitably overshadowed by Dean's enormous success.

Adam collapsed and suffered a stroke. The reconciliation of father and son was wholly unconvincing, yet undeniably poignant, and with the help of Rosenman's score, the death scene was played for its full tear-jerking possibilities.

Julie Harris, once again so affecting in her love and concern for Adam and Cal, set the whole scene up, reaching out to father and son. 'It's awful not to be loved. It's the worst thing in the world. It makes you mean, violent and cruel.' She begged Adam to give his son a sign of his love, to make Cal a man, whole and strong. 'Let him know you love him.'

Harris, with her inner grace, meek yet strong, was wonderful. She deserved an Oscar nomination for her performance as much as Dean did for his.

66 Nothing captured or came close to being the true Dean as *East of Eden*, nothing… I could not believe that Kazan had got so close, to have been able to use Dean himself so thoroughly. It could have been Jimmy's own story.

William Bast in interview in *Hollywood: The Rebels*

66 Dean had no technique to speak of… On my film, Jimmy would either get the scene right immediately, without any detailed direction – that was ninety-five percent of the time – or he couldn't get it all… I doubt if Jimmy would have ever got through *East of Eden* except for an angel on our set. Her name was Julie Harris, and she was goodness itself with Dean, kind and patient, and everlastingly sympathetic.

Elia Kazan *A Life*

66 I was out of the country during the filming. When I returned, the whole thing was finished and cut and the music set in. I was able to see it as one piece. And I was overwhelmed with what they had done. I think it might be the best film I ever saw. I don't think the fact of my having written the book has anything to do with that connection. They have not translated my book. Translations rarely succeed. But they have taken the theme and story and set them down in a different medium. What I saw was familiar and true but fresh and new to me. It is a fine thing, and I am grateful.

John Steinbeck *New York Herald Tribune*

66 Jimmy had only to act himself. But that is a difficult role even for an experienced actor to play. A rebel at heart, he approached everything with a chip on his shoulder. The Method had encouraged this truculent spirit. Jimmy never knew his lines before he walked on the set, rarely had command of them when the camera rolled and even if he had was often inaudible. Simple technicalities, such as moving on cue and finding his mark, were beneath his consideration.

Raymond Massey *A Hundred Different Lives*

66 But the box office asset that is most important is the debut, in the leading role of a handsome and dynamic young actor named James Dean. This is the boy who is apt to captivate the typical movie fans whether or not they like tragic stories. He is that rare thing, a young actor who is a great actor and the troubled eloquence with which he puts over the problems of misunderstood youth may lead to his being accepted by young audiences as a sort of symbol of their generation. He's the only player I have ever seen who'd be completely right for Romeo. It is inevitable that he will be compared to Marlon Brando, though he is no carbon copy of that capable player. He has a completely individual screen personality. If the film is to reap the profits it deserves, no time should be lost in giving him a big fan magazine buildup, not because he is trivial, but because it's the quickest way to rally young people to his support.

Jack Moffitt *Hollywood Reporter*

66 This young actor, who is here doing his first big screen stint, is a mass of histrionic gingerbread. He scuffs his feet, he whirls, he pouts, he sputters, he leans against walls, he rolls his eyes, he swallows his words, he ambles slack-kneed – all like Marlon Brando used to. Never have we seen a performer so clearly follow another's style. Mr Kazan should be spanked for permitting him to do such a sophomoric thing. Whatever there might be of reasonable torment in this youngster is buried beneath the clumsy display.

Bosley Crowther *New York Times*

James Dean and
Raymond Massey in
East of Eden

66 Dean tries so hard to find the part in himself that he often forgets to put himself into the part. But no matter what he is doing, he has the presence of a young lion and the same sense of danger about him. His eye is as empty as an animal's and he lolls and gallops with the innocence and grace of an animal.

Time

66 He looks like a miniature Gregory Peck, but he has obviously been going to a few movies featuring Marlon Brando. Or maybe he's just been going to the movies. At any rate he represents a school of acting that might be described as unpredictable. There is no telling

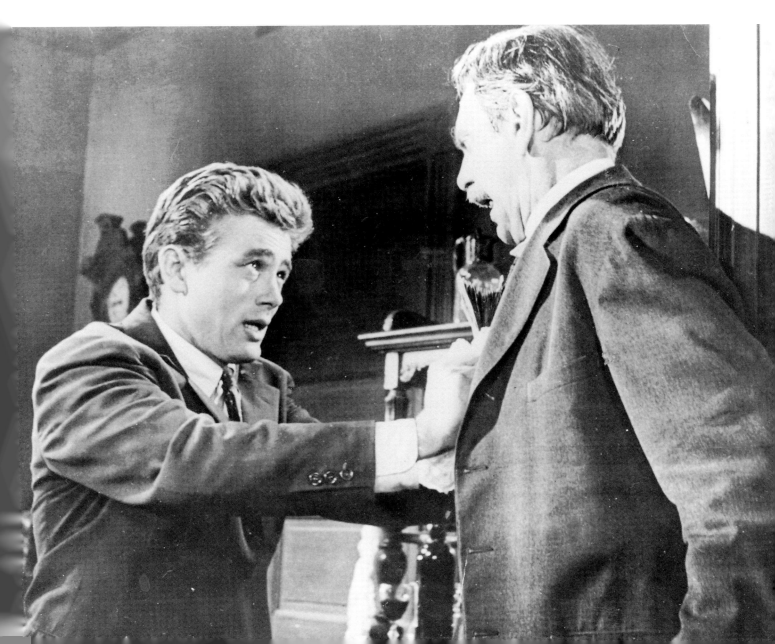

how he will react to any situation. Sometimes he jumps up and down like a kangaroo, sometimes he giggles like a lunatic, and sometimes he is surly and offended. He's a hard man to decipher.

John McCarten *New Yorker*

❝ *East of Eden* is the first film to give us a Baudelarian hero, fascinated by vice and contrast, loving the family and hating the family at one and the same time.

François Truffaut

❝ He is another landmark in the deterioration of the hero. For Hollywood through the years has certainly changed its mind about the ideal male. He is no longer handsome, suave, daring and romantic. Now he is sullen, aggressive, inarticulate, and muscle-bound... James Dean in *East of Eden* is of the juvenile delinquent school. He has the slouching grace of a tired cat and eyes that stare with the compelling magnetism of a deep and empty cave. When he is emotionally disturbed he flails his arms about like a windmill. But he comes out of the screen at you like a hurtling panther, and women will undoubtedly be thrilled to have him in their laps.

Milton Shulman *Sunday Express*

Richard Davalos, James Dean and Jo Van Fleet in *East of Eden*

❝ Cal is interestingly played by James Dean, a young actor whose ability is strikingly in evidence, although at the moment too transparently applied to the rather gratuitous task of imitating Marlon Brando. James Dean has been cheapened into a less important sort of myth, but the performance survives with extraordinary force. If ever an errant generation threw up an expression of itself, it was him: like Cain, he has the look of a fugitive and a vagabond in the earth.

Penelope Gilliatt *Observer*

Rebel Without a Cause

Director	Nicholas Ray
Studio	Warner Bros
Release	1955
Producer	David Weisbart
Screenplay	Stewart Stern
Adaptation	Irving Shulman
From a story by	Nicholas Ray
Photography	Ernest Haller
Music	Leonard Rosenman

*Nominated for an Oscar by the Academy of Motion Pictures Arts and Sciences.

Role	Cast
Jim	James Dean
Judy	Natalie Wood*
Jim's Father	Jim Backus
Jim's Mother	Ann Doran
Judy's Mother	Rochelle Hudson
Judy's Father	William Hopper
Plato	Sal Mineo*
Buzz	Corey Allen
Goon	Dennis Hopper
Ray	Edward Platt
Mil	Steffi Sidney
Negro Woman	Marietta Canty
Jim's Grandma	Virginia Brissac
Helen	Beverley Long
Lecturer	Ian Wolfe
Crunch	Frank Mazzola
Gene	Robert Foulk
Cookie	Jack Simmons
Harry	Tom Bernard
Moose	Nick Adams
Chick	Jack Grinnage
Cliff	Clifford Morris

Poster for
Rebel Without a Cause

❝ Dean was a model of adolescence in general and American adolescence in particular. He was someone, who seemed to symbolize the doubts and aspirations of his generation.

Nicholas Ray

Rebel Without a Cause began shooting on 28 March 1955 as a modest B picture in black and white. Four days later Warner Bros ordered the existing footage to be scrapped. The budget was then substantially increased and filming continued in CinemaScope, stereophone and WarnerColor. The reason for Warner's change of mind was the release of *East of Eden* and the realization of James Dean's new potential at the box office.

Director Nicholas Ray, with screenwriter Stewart Stern, had travelled all over America interviewing hundreds of police officers, judges, youth leaders and juvenile welfare officers to collect material for the film. They had observed at first hand the operation of a juvenile gang and spent many days at Los Angeles Juvenile Court watching young boys and girls being charged. They discussed the psychological motivation of the characters with Professor Douglas Kelley, professor of criminology at the University of California, and engaged a former real-life gang member, Frank Mazzola, as consultant and actor.

Rebel Without a Cause was a study of alienated American youth told from their point of view. The parents were put on trial and found guilty. 'There are more delinquent parents than there are delinquent children,' said Ray, his sympathies over-weighted in favour of the kids. As one wag remarked, 'Few pictures have given so clear a picture of how not to bring up mum and dad.' (A good spanking was what they needed).

The film was a serious attempt to tackle a serious problem and Ray had insisted that all the characters should be based on real-life cases. Audiences were thus provided with a commercial mix of social commentary, psychological study, family drama, and violence. The commentary aimed at realism and honesty. The psychology tended to be marred by a text-book glibness, the theatrics

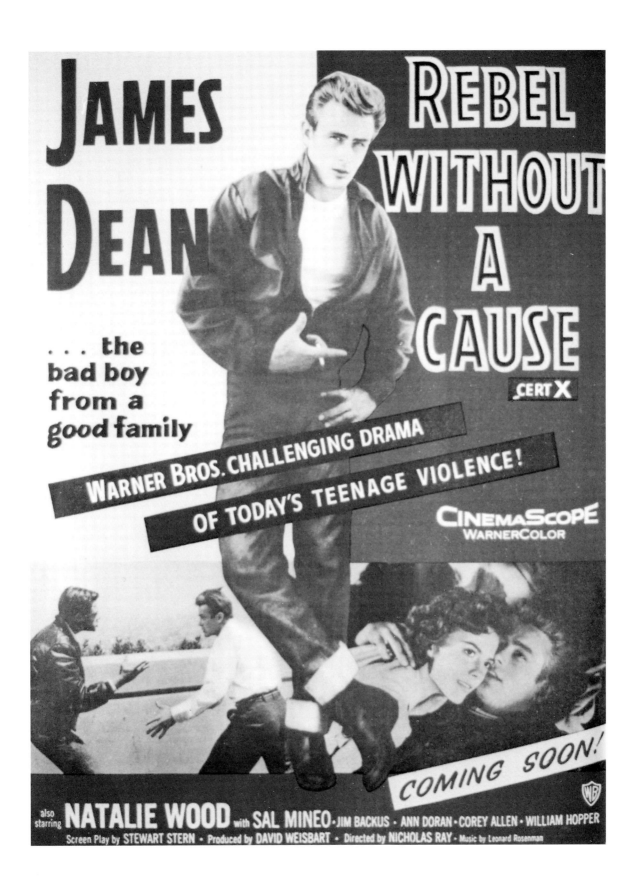

degenerated too often into hysteria, but the violence was dangerous and graphic enough to produce an outcry.

However, *Rebel Without a Cause* was not another *Blackboard Jungle*, nor was it another *The Wild One* (both released in the same year); and it was all the more shocking precisely because it wasn't. Poverty was not the problem. The parents were the well-to-do middle-class, living in suburbia in pleasant, comfortable, well-appointed homes, and their children went to a modern school and drove their own cars.

The screenplay concentrated on three cases histories. The introductions at a police station were skilfully edited so that the separate stories were linked, the camera moving between the characters, concentrating on one case history, while keeping the other two cases in the background and often within the same frame. Ray's crisp direction made excellent use of the CinemaScope screen.

Jim Stark (James Dean) was a sensitive 17-year-old lad craving for love and rebelling against middle-class conformity. He was in a new town, making a new start at a new school. Materially he had everything; spiritually he had nothing.

His parents were crude and clichéd caricatures out of Freud. Mr Stark (Jim Backus), physically flabby, mentally shillyshallying, was a self-deprecating, hen-pecked weakling. Mrs Stark (Ann Doran) was an emotional blackmailing shrew. 'Remember how I almost died giving birth to him? How can you say I don't care?' she screamed during one heated argument. Mother and father bickered constantly. Grandma (Virginia Brissac) was a coiffured old witch and Jim felt somebody ought to poison her Epsom salts.

The second child was 17-year-old Judy (Natalie Wood in her first grown-up part) whose father (William Hopper) could not cope with the fact that his daughter was no longer a little girl. He was so worried by his incestuous feelings for her that he had transferred his affections to his young son. Embarrassed by any displays of affection, he smacked her across the face when she tried to kiss him. Judy's mother (Rochelle Hudson), a cardboard cutout, barely existing in her own right, played a supporting role to her husband.

Judy was convinced her father must hate her. ('He called me a dirty tramp, my own father!') She had been found wandering the streets at one o'clock in the morning, so he might have had a point. However, this being the 1950s, the film censor had insisted there must be no suggestion whatsoever of a minor being promiscuous and soliciting.

The third child was 15-year-old Plato, deeply unhappy and possibly mentally ill. He had run amok with a gun and killed a litter of puppies. His parents were divorced. His mother had deserted him on his birthday to see her lover. His father, a Greek tycoon, had abandoned him totally and communicated only by cheque once a month. Unloved and friendless, he lived alone in a large house, cared for only by a black housekeeper (Marietta Canty).

Plato was played by 16-year-old Sal Mineo, who had first come to the notice of Hollywood when he had acted the young prince in Rodgers and Hammerstein's *The King and I* on Broadway. Mineo was so obviously so much younger than the other actors playing the students that it was implausible that he would have gone anywhere near them.

The opening scene found Jim Stark lying inebriated in the middle of the road, playing with a toy monkey and curling up next to it in a foetal position, his hands between his legs. It was irritating that the image of the two chimps side by side should have been spoiled by the credit titles being superimposed on them.

The moment the credits ended, the film cut to Jim being carried into the police station by

a police officer and charged with being drunk. Ticklish, he giggled as he was being searched, a characteristic and engaging touch on Dean's part, instantly confirming his credentials as Method Actor. The giggling stopped when a cop tried to take the monkey away. His drunken seriousness about keeping the toy was both funny and true.

Soon afterwards there was an image of Jim sprawled all over a chair imitating a police siren. Dean, 23 years old in real life, looked all of 18 and acted even younger, a naughty, silly, sozzled teenager up well past his bedtime. The arrival of his quarrelling parents sobered him up instantly.

'YOU'RE TEARING ME APART!' he cried. It is one of the cinema's great cries of pain and a whole generation of teenagers immediately identified with it. It became the film's most famous single line of dialogue, often quoted and much imitated.

The welfare officer (Edward Platt), who worked in the juvenile division, decided that this was a good moment to get him away from his parents. Alone in his office Jim tried to sock him on the jaw and failed pathetically, ending up on the floor. The officer suggested that he might like to vent his anger on his desk instead. Jim, bemused by the idea, hit it, kicked it, pummelled it hard. The desk retaliated.

Warner Bros's press office took the opportunity for a bit of publicity and issued a statement: 'James Dean suffered a badly bruised right hand today while doing a scene. Dean slapped his right fist into the side of a desk a little harder than the script called for. He was taken to an emergency hospital where x rays revealed no broken bones but he will have to keep his hand wrapped in an elastic bandage for at least a week.'

The interview with the welfare officer continued. Jim complained that his parents didn't understand him and that they never had. (So what's new?) He peered through the eye-hole in the door to observe them still quarrelling and gave the shutter a twirl. (Dean always used any objects that were around to his advantage, invariably upstaging the other actors.) Jim admitted he was ashamed of the way his father let himself be eaten alive by his mother and that he didn't ever want to be like him. He longed for his dad to have the guts to knock his mom cold.

It has often been said that *Rebel Without a Cause* invented the modern high school teenager and it isn't difficult to understand how a young audience was able to relate to Dean, especially when he was saying things like: 'Boy, if I had one day when I didn't have to be all confused and didn't have to feel I was ashamed of everything. If I felt that I belonged some place…'

On his first day at school, one of the classes took place in the planetarium. 'In all the immensity of our universe and the galaxies beyond, the earth will not be missed,' intoned the lecturer, developing one of the film's themes. 'Through the infinite reaches of space, the problems of man seem trivial and naive indeed and man existing alone seems himself an episode of little consequence.'

During the lecture Jim made mooing sounds, a childish and embarrassing attempt to ingratiate himself with the gang sitting in front of him, which backfired. They were waiting for him when he came out of the building. Their leader, Buzz (Corey Allen), was the sort of guy who slashed the tyres of students' cars and if he was challenged produced a switch-knife. The gang members (amongst them 17-year-old Dennis Hopper) were mere background figures, not characterized and generally looking too old.

Jim had been in enough trouble in his previous schools and genuinely wanted to make a fresh start, but when they accused him of being 'chicken' he was unable to walk away. Buzz mocked him, playing toreador to his unwilling bull, forcing him to pick up the knife he had thrown down. The fight, realistically choreographed, was heavily censored in Britain.

Buzz challenged Jim to a chicken run and Jim accepted without having any idea what a chicken run was. He came home to find his father in a frilly apron on his hands and knees cleaning up a mess on the landing.

'Better clean it up before she sees it,' said dad.

'Let her see it,' said Jim.

Jim turned to his father for advice. Mr Stark, as always totally incapable of giving a direct answer, took circumlocution to new lengths and waffled on about considering the pros and cons and making lists, saying Jim would laugh about it in ten years. ('TEN YEARS!' cried Dean.)

Jim decided there was only one thing to be done and he did it. He got out of his jacket, his trousers and shirt (a rare chance to see Dean bare-chested) and he put on a T-shirt, blue jeans and a red nylon windcheater. Clearly, he meant business. Years later singer Adam Faith would remember how he and thousands of other kids had gone straight out and bought themselves levis and red windcheaters.

The chicken run, which took place on a moonlit night, was a duel with stolen cars fought out on a promontory, a contest of nerves in which the drivers raced to the edge of a cliff. The first one to jump out of his car was 'chicken'.

There was a gesture of friendship between the two combatants before battle commenced.

'You know something? I like you,' said Buzz.

'Why do we do this? asked Jim.

'You gotta to do something, don't you?' he replied in one of the key lines of the screenplay. For so many youngsters in the 1950s (unlike the 1960s) there was nothing for them to get

James Dean in
Rebel Without a Cause

emotional about. They were indeed rebels without causes.

The two teenagers rubbed their hands with dirt to get a better grip on the wheels of their stolen cars. All the other cars were lined up either side of them, the passage between forming a runway to the cliff's edge.

'Hit your lights!' screamed Judy, Buzz's girl friend.

Buzz (who had been combing his hair in an arrogant manner before setting off) got his sleeve caught in the door handle and was unable to get out of the car. He went over the cliff edge, screaming as he plunged to his death on the rocks below. The sea (and Leonard Rosenman's music on the soundtrack) churned away. The sheer stupidity of chicken runs was nothing new to American audiences. They had been hitting the headlines fairly regularly; but with Dean so recently dead, the scene took on an added frisson, a macabre irony.

Jim returned home, took a bottle of milk out of the fridge and rubbed his brow and cheek, just the sort of thing a Method Actor would do, but at the time it seemed totally original, an unexpected bit of business, which has proved to be one of Dean's most abiding images.

His father was slumped in a chair in front of a blank television screen. Jim lay down on the settee. The entrance of his mother down the stairs was seen from his angle, the camera doing an 180 degree turn.

'I've got to talk to somebody,' he said. 'I want a direct answer. I'm in trouble.'

Mr Stark agreed with everything Jim said before he had even said it. Jim went berserk. 'YOU'RE NOT LISTENING!' he screamed. He said he was going to the police. His parents wanted him to stay home and not get involved.

'But I am involved. We're all involved. A boy died tonight. Mom, just once I want to do something right and I don't want you to run away from me again. Dad, stand up for me. STAND UP!'

The scene was played out on the staircase so that Ray could get the extreme camera angles he wanted to increase the tension. Jim then dragged his father to his feet, down the stairs across the room, on to a chair, which toppled over, and attempted to throttle him. 'TALK TO ME!'

The melodrama did not stop there. Jim kicked a painting of mom, which was somewhat strangely off the wall, lying besides the French windows, just waiting to be kicked in the face by her son before he made his exit through the windows, bumping into the frame as he went. Bumping-into-furniture exits were Dean's trademark, justified by the emotion just spent, but also, perhaps, because he was blind as a bat without his glasses and couldn't see where he was going.

The whole scene, performed by the actors at the tops of their voices, was like a scene in a play. (*Rebel Without a Cause* would be turned into a play in 1958.) It was Jim's fight with his father which got the film its X certificate in Britain, ensuring it opened in London at the London Pavilion, home to sensational movies. It didn't get an AA until its re-release 21 years later.

Jim went to the police station to give himself up but the welfare officer who had befriended him was not there. He found Judy instead and they had an intimate scene which ended with him giving her a peck.

'Why did you do that for?'

'Felt like it.'

'Your lips are soft.'

They decided not to go home and hid in a deserted mansion. The mansion had already been used in Billy Wilder's *Sunset Boulevard*. Film buffs would not have been surprised if

Norma Desmond had come sweeping down the staircase saying, 'I'm ready for my close-up, Mr de Mille.'

Meanwhile Plato had been attacked by three members of Buzz's gang who wanted to know where Jim was. Pausing only to grab a gun from his under his pillow, he rushed to warn Jim that the gang was after him.

Jim and Judy pretended to be an estate agent showing newly-weds round the mansion: 'We don't encourage children, they're too noisy and troublesome... so annoying when they cry... As you can see, the nursery is far away from the rest of the house and if you have children you'll find this a wonderful arrangement... they can carry on and you'll never notice... if you lock them in,

you'll never have to see them again, much less talk to them... Nobody talks to children. They just tell them.'

Dean did a quick party-imitation of the short-sighted, rasping Mr Magoo, very much a private joke for co-stars, director and crew, and only appreciated if cinemagoers knew Jim Backus voiced the Magoo cartoons.

The three youngsters played in and around the empty pool. (It was the pool in which William Holden, in his role of Norma Desmond's lover, had ended up murdered.) The fun and games got more and more childish until Jim and Judy were playing mummy and daddy, pretending to be surrogate parents to Plato. The idyll, which should have been poignant, wasn't, and came across as bad

Jim Backus, James Dean and Ann Doran in Rebel Without a Cause

Sal Mineo, James Dean and Natalie Wood in *Rebel Without a Cause*

Jean Cocteau, candelabra and all.

Plato fell asleep. His 'new parents' (no different to his real parents) immediately abandoned him to explore the house. Judy wanted Jim to be brave, strong, a man who could be gentle and sweet. Head to head, their faces filling the whole of the CinemaScope screen, they agreed they were not going to be lonely ever again.

'I love you, Jim, I really mean it.'

They kissed. Whatever else they might have done took place off-screen. Nicholas Ray said *Romeo and Juliet* had always struck him as the best play ever written about 'juvenile delinquents'. However, if he had wanted a Romeo and Juliet feeling about Jim and Judy and their families, he didn't get it.

Meanwhile the gang of three had arrived and Plato was attacked again. Firing his gun and wounding one of the boys, he made a dash for it, pursued by Jim and Judy.

'Why did you run out on me? Why did you leave me?' he asked when they finally caught

up with him in the planetarium.

Ray, skilfully maintaining the tension and pace, played out the final scene on the steps leading up to the planetarium, a convenient stage for any Greek classical drama, the lighting, in this instance, provided by the headlights of the encircling police cars.

Plato was killed when he emerged from the building and panicking, drew his gun. Jim (his character transformed from social misfit to responsible citizen in one night) had done everything a man could have done to avoid the violent end. But how were the trigger-happy police to know that inside the planetarium he had tricked Plato into lending him the gun and had secretly emptied the magazine before he had handed it back?

'I'VE GOT THE BULLET!' Jim screamed, his hands outstretched, spread-eagled in agony, knowing that he was in part responsible for Plato's death. Dean was never afraid of the big, hysterical gesture. He made slow wounded movements round the dead body, laughing/crying at Plato's odd socks. The laughter-in-tears would have been very familiar to anybody who had seen Dean's work on television.

Romantic music had played on the soundtrack the first time Plato had seen Jim. 'He's my best friend', he had told Judy at the chicken run. Sunday, he's going to take me hunting and fishing.' Had Jim really promised this? Or was Plato living in a fantasy world? It wasn't clear when he had had time to get to know Jim.

Plato (who had a picture of Alan Ladd in his locker) was obviously infatuated with Jim. The homo-eroticism, one-sided, one-handed, was not reciprocated. The love was not even acknowledged until the very end when Jim gave the dead Plato his red nylon jacket. (No man has greater love than he lay down his red nylon jacket for another man.) At the police station some 24 hours earlier, Jim had tried to lend him his jacket but it had been refused. Now he zipped up Plato's dead body in it.

Scriptwriter Stewart Stern, in an interview in the film documentary, *The Celluloid Closet* (a compilation of overt and covert homosexual scenes in the movies), had said that if he were writing the screenplay in the 1990s he would have made it much more explicit and that Plato would have emerged the true rebel.

Strictly speaking, from a truly tragic point of view, it was Jim who should have been killed. Better still both Jim and Judy, the star-cross'd lovers, should have died, but clearly the studio didn't want to kill off their new star and risk killing the box office, so the supporting actor was killed instead.

James Dean and Nicholas Ray on the set of Rebel Without a Cause

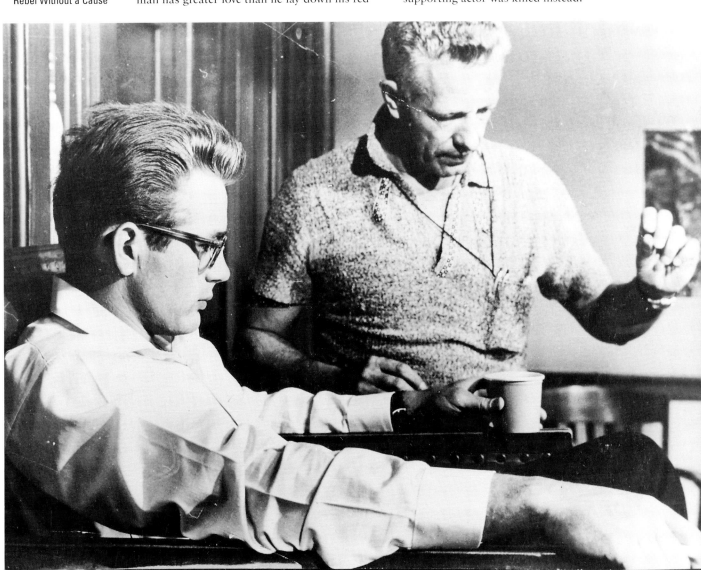

The final moments were very contrived.
'Help me, dad,' pleaded Jim.

'You can depend on me,' said Mr Stark. 'Trust me. I'll try and be as strong as you want me to be.' (Fat, flabby chance of that.)

Mom and dad gave each other the sort of look which said we've made it up, we'll never quarrel ever again, and we'll be good parents from now on. The happy ending was as false as it was embarrassing and it was left to the distraught housekeeper/nanny, in her role of Greek chorus, to try and give the ending some genuine dignity. 'Poor baby,' she said (referring to Plato) 'just got nobody'.

As the credit titles rolled, a solitary figure walked to the planetarium. It was Nicholas Ray. What was going to do when he got there?

Sal Mineo, surprisingly, got a nomination for an Oscar. So, surprisingly, did Natalie Wood. Neither of them won, losing respectively to Jack Lemmon in Mr Roberts and Jo Van Fleet in *East of Eden*. Dean wasn't nominated, presumably because he had already been nominated for *East of Eden*.

" I know that if anyone was ever dedicated to the art of acting, it was Jimmy. He had the greatest power of concentration I have ever encountered... He prepared for his scene in his dressingroom listening to the 'Ride of Valkyrie'... He stormed out, strode onto the set, did the scene, which was practically a seven minute monologue, in one take, so brilliantly that even the hard-boiled crew cheered and applauded. He played that scene so intensely that he broke two small bones in his hand when he beat the desk which he practically demolished... threw me down a flight of stairs, across the living room, into a chair, which went over backwards and tried to choke me to death... I was two hundred

pounds of dead weight. He could not have weighed more than 140 pounds and this boy carried, dragged me down the stairs, across the room and into the chair over and over again... Due to the tremendous intensity with which Jimmy approached his work, people got the impression that he was rude, ill-tempered and surly... After I got to know him I realized he was very shy, although essentially a very warm person.

Jim Backus

" In *East of Eden*, under Elia Kazan's direction, the 24-year-old actor was thought to be doing a Marlon Brando. But freed from Kazan's evaluations of character, this resemblance vanishes. Almost free of mannerisms under Ray's pacing, Dean is very effective as a boy groping for adjustment to people. As a 'farewell' performance he leaves behind, with this film, genuine artistic regret, for here was a talent which might have touched the heights. His actor's capacity to get inside the skin of youthful pain, torment and bewilderment is not often encountered.

Land *Variety*

" His rare talent and appealing personality even shine through this turgid melodrama.

William Dinsser *New York Herald Tribune*

" However we do wish the young actors, including Mr Dean, had not been so intent on imitating Marlon Brando in varying degrees. The tendency, possibly typical of the behavior of certain youths, may therefore be a subtle commentary but it grows monotonous.

Bosley Crowther *New York Times*

" James Dean gives a performance wholly his own, more electric to my mind than any of Marlon Brando's. His recent death is a real tragedy for Hollywood in its present mood.

William Whitebait *New Statesman and Nation*

James Dean and
Natalie Wood in
Rebel Without A Cause

66 It is a superb portrayal of a youth's misdirected adolescence – emotional, even hysterical, where the script demands; but mostly controlled with a keen sense of quiet, dramatic tension. Above all, Dean's own personality – with its groping, inarticulate appeal – takes complete command of our sympathies. This is a performance with much of Marlon Brando's dramatic power, nearly all his technique – and an innate, sensitive charm which Brando has never shown.

Harold Conway *Daily Sketch*

66 James Dean, alas, is dead. But his ghost on the screen in what was only his second film will remain among the immortals of the cinema. On his first appearance I described him as being 'the best bad boy since Brando'. I think in this film that he transcends even that exceptional actor. He has the same sulky, stumbling grace of movement and slack-lipped, word-swallowing eloquence. He grunts are more rhetorical than most actors' speeches. But he manages also to suggest the soul beneath the skin, the emotion beneath the lethargy. He might also be described as the intellectual who seems often to be struggling to escape from within Brando's Napoleonic thug exterior. And with his giggles and rages, his depressions and intoxications, his sudden bursts of passion and his long slumps of boredom, he creates a portrait of a baffled young man in three dimensions.

Alan Brien *Evening Standard*

66 Mr Dean's bruised sensibility and the inarticulate staccato of his speech make him an extremely expressive figure as the misunderstood adolescent.

Derek Granger *Financial Times*

66 A performance by James Dean as Rebel Number One which leaves us more than ever convinced that his death last year robbed screen and stage of a sensitive, individual and fast-growing actor.

C. A. Lejeune *Observer*

66 The film, like adolescence itself, moves by fits and starts, now deliberately inarticulate, now breaking into a burst of frenzied expression. It uses the condensed language of verse rather than the relaxed rhythms of prose, and James Dean wonderfully enters into the mood and intention of the whole. His Jim is a creature trying desperately to communicate his need and his loneliness, and all that he can manage is a kind of inspired yet jerky, intermittent, uncertain form of morse-code. It is at once like the efforts of the adolescent to understand, too much, and not enough.

The Times

66 James Dean is, of course, the most conspicuous of the three crazy, mixed-up kids and his acting is the keynote. He puts on, certainly, an astonishing show of gangling, gauche, mumbling virtuosity – never a sentence completed, never a movement made without a stumble or at least a hesitation. It is most impressive – but not altogether convincing. Or at least this performance's powers of conviction, however they may seem to an American audience, do not quite survive the Atlantic crossing.

Manchester Guardian

66 Among several fine performances, one is unforgettable in its subtlety and strength, its power to suggest, by a shrug, an awkward gesture, a hesitant word, an unexpectedly charming smile or suddenly unleashed fury, all the loneliness of the young, their dreams and agonised confusions. I have seen many interpretations of Hollywood's pet character,

Sal Mineo, James Dean and Natalie Wood in *Rebel Without a Cause*

the mixed-up kid, which means anybody under 40. I still say this a *tour de force*.

Campbell Dixon *Daily Telegraph*

❝ Only a superb interpretation could have given this the texture of a deeply corrosive, psychic disorder, and James Dean (whose second film this was), magnificently achieved it… The actor movingly captures the conflict in all its multiple evasions, betrayals, sudden giggling release of tension, and agonised deadlock, and achieves a genuinely poetic account of a modern misfit.

Derek Prouse *Sight and Sound*

❝ There has been no player of his or any other generation to rival his interpretation of the violent desperation of youth… after three decades, it is Dean who stands out: the tireless body, the insistent face, the sense of indignation with life. For once you can understand mass devotion, for once it seems to be expanded on genuine gifts. I still think there was something in his make-up waiting to develop. I still think he had a kind of genius.

Dilys Powell *Sunday Times*

❝ *Rebel Without a Cause* will remain a masterpiece, because it is the American cinema's only Greek Tragedy.

William Faulkner

101

Giant

Director	George Stevens
Studio	Warner Bros
Release	1956
Producers	George Stevens and
	Henry Ginsberg
Screenplay	Fred Guiol* and Ivan Moffat*
From the novel by	Edna Ferber
Music	Dimitri Tiomkin*
Photography	William C. Mellor
Editors	William Hornbeck,*
	Philip W. Anderson,*
	Fred Robson*
Art Direction	Boris Leven*
Costume Design	Moss Mabry* and
	Ralph S. Hurst*

*nominated for Oscars by the Academy of Motion Pictures Arts and Sciences.

Role	Cast
Leslie Benedict	Elizabeth Taylor
Bick Benedict	Rock Hudson*
Jett Rink	James Dean*
Vashti Snythe	Jane Withers
Uncle Bawley	Chill Wills
Luz Benedict	Mercedes McCambridge*
Luz Benedict II	Carroll Barker
Jordon Benedict III	Dennis Hopper
Mrs Horace Lynnton	Judith Evelyn
Dr Horace Lynnton	Paul Fix
Sir David Karfrey	Rodney Taylor
Bob Dace	Earl Holliman
Pinky Snythe	Robert Nichols
Old Polo	Alexander Scourby
Angel Obregon III	Sal Mineo
Judy Benedict	Fran Bennett
Whiteside	Charles Watts
Juana	Elsa Cardenas
Lacey Lynnton	Carolyn Craig
Bale Lynch	Monte Halo
Adarene Clinch	Mary Ann Edwards
Gabe Targot	Sheb Wooley
Angel Obregon I	Victor Millan
Sarge	Mickey Simpson
Mrs Obregon	Pilar del Rey
Dr Guerra	Maurice Jara
Lona Lano	Noreen Nash
Swazey	Napoloeon Whiting
Lupe	Tim Menard
Watts	Ray Whiting

James Dean in *Giant*

66 Edna Ferber can always be relied on for a good story interwoven with fascinating information and sound moral judgements on the shortcomings as well as the virtues of her country and its history.

Marghanita Laski *Spectator*

Giant, Edna Ferber's best-selling novel of 1952, was the story of how Texas became Texas. 'Miss Ferber', wrote John Barkham in *The New York Times*, 'makes it very clear that she doesn't like the Texas she writes about, and it's a cinch that when Texans read about what she has written about them they won't like Miss Ferber either.'

The lone star state was turned into a symbol, a *giant* symbol, for all that was least estimable in America: its money-grabbing materialism, its thick-skinned self-interest, its profligacy and vulgarity, its lowbrowism, its snobbery and racism, its narrow-mindedness its self-satisfied isolationism, and its spiritual impoverishment.

The novel, a long, slow, rambling and overwrought family saga, sprawled across three generations. Though it was strongly denied, the two leading characters bore a remarkable resemblance to a real and readily recognisable couple. 'It is about as difficult to identify the characters and places in *Giant* as it would be to recognize the Washington monument if it were painted purple,' wrote William Kittrell in *Saturday Review*.

In the 1950s size was Hollywood's answer in the fight against television and at 3 hours 18 minutes, *Giant* was among the longest films ever made. (If it were made today, it would no doubt be a mini-series on television.) Production values were high and William C. Mellor's camerawork was excellent, capturing the atmosphere of the great open spaces with panoramic vistas of dusty plains and oil derricks masturbating

103

away in unionism. George Stevens, who believed that 25 per cent of the creative process took place in the editing room, had taken a year to edit the film. (He might with advantage have taken out another 30 minutes.) Though *Giant* won Stevens an Oscar for best director, it is not in the same class as his previous films, *A Place in the Sun* and *Shane*.

The trailer had promised 'a century of stormy passions, deep human understanding and love, love, always love, powerful, unquestioning, constant', but what this had to with the film was anybody's guess.

The screenplay stuck pretty close to the novel. Bick Benedict (Rock Hudson) was a rich Texan cattle baron, a handsome, proud, perverse man who treated women as second-class citizens. His intelligent and sophisticated wife, Leslie (Elizabeth Taylor) from Virginia, equally strong-willed and high-spirited, rebelled against her subservient role. Liberal and humane, she found the contrast between the rich and the poor unacceptable and hated the way the Texans treated the Mexican Indians.

James Dean was cast as Jett Rink, a poor ranchhand who worked for the Benedict family. His opening shot was a close-up of his face. He was wearing a cowboy hat and his eyes were in shadow. A cigarette dangled from his mouth. He stood by a broken down car in his jeans, watching Bick carry his bride over the threshold. Bick was under the impression he had fired Rink.

Jett was insolent, scornful. 'Simmer down,' he drawled. 'Tell me who is the boss and I'll be glad to do anything they want me to do!' As he made to shake the bride's hand, Bick cut him short, ordering him to fix a truck. He departed, surly-like. 'Ain't nobody king in this country,' he muttered, 'ain't nobody, whatever they might be thinking.'

Bick gave a barbecue to introduce his wife

to his friends, associates and neighbours. Jett remained on the periphery, a lonely outsider, stroking the rump of a stallion, unable to enter the crude, noisy society he despised so much yet wished so much to be a part of.

There was the classic and much reproduced image of Dean lounging in the back seat of a car with his legs on the headrest of the front seat, his stetson on his feet. In the background was the Gothic mansion in which the Benedicts lived. The shot looked like a painting by Andrew Wyeth. Jett looked like he was biding his time. A haunting solo played on the soundtrack.

Some time later driving Mrs Benedict back home after a day on the range, an amusing exchange took place between them at a water-pump where they had stopped for a drink.

'I'm not too awful bad now,' he confided. 'I've got a few friends.'

Mrs Benedict assured him she liked him.

'I like you, too,' he admitted. 'I guess you're about the best looking girl we've seen around here in a long time. I think the prettiest, I've seen down here.'

She thanked him and then (teasing him) she said that, with his permission, she was going to tell her husband about his compliment and that she had met with his approval. Dean, all cute and sheepish, shambled around, mumbling, shaking his head, not thinking that was a good idea at all. The humour of the scene was beautifully underplayed by him and Taylor.

In the novel Jett Rink was much more of a threatening sexual danger. Ferber described him as 'a brute... savage... dirty, belligerent, irresponsible, sadistic... a sullen loutish kind of boy, who bore a grudge against the world.' Dean concentrated on the sullenness and the grudge.

Bick Benedict had an older sister, Luz, played by Mercedes McCambridge, who shirted, spurred, harsh-voiced, and tough as old boots, looked as if she had been on the range

James Dean and
Rock Hudson in *Giant*

business associates assured him. Jett, the little boy patronized by the big guys, slouched in his chair and went along with them. Barely raising his head, his eyes flicking from face to face, he laughed, winked, muttered, and played with his lariat. Some (including Rock Hudson) have seen the rope-play as a bit of 'business' to upstage the other actors (and it may well have been) but the scene was Dean's and it was totally in keeping with Rink's character. The interaction between Rink and the pompously jolly and utterly phoney Judge Whiteside (Charles Watts) was perfectly gauged by both actors.

Jett thanked them for their generosity but said he preferred to gamble and keep what Luz had given him. As he left the room he turned and made a slicing gesture with his hand, signalling goodbye and good rinse.

Just in case cinemagoers hadn't fully appreciated the significance of what had just happened, the message was underlined. As Jett walked through the outer crowded room, he passed a woman who was saying, 'There's only one thing on this earth more important than money and that's land.' This statement was then clinched by a neat bit of comedy. Mrs Benedict was talking to a couple who had had a run of luck. Their gusher had come in, bringing them in a million. 'A million gallons?' she inquired. 'No, a million dollars,' they replied. 'A million dollars a year!' she exclaimed. She was wrong again. They meant a million dollars a month.

The next image of Dean was as a lone figure in a vast landscape, silhouetted against an enormous sky, pacing out his land in huge nursery-like strides, his arms swinging by his side. It remains one of the most memorable and enduring images of the film. The sequence ended with the boy-king climbing his castle (a broken down windmill) to survey the land he had inherited. Dimitri Tiomkin's Oscar-

all her life. When Jett and Mrs Benedict returned, they found Luz was dying. She had been thrown by the stallion she had been brutally breaking in.

Jett stood in the open doorway, leaning on the portal, much of his face in shadow, looking like the young cowhand he was. There was no dialogue, only his gulping Adam's apple to register his grief. He sat down on the steps, his face now totally in shadow, his head in his hands, a forlorn figure, who had lost the only friend and family he had.

In her will Luz had left him a bit of land and the Benedicts wanted it back. They offered him $1200, twice as much as 'the no-good little water hole' was worth, so Bick's nominated score, alternating between the romantic and the thumping, produced a a rousing hymn-like sound, which would become associated with the oil he would later find.

Time passed. Jett was discovered at a pump with his dog, his sole companion. He fired his gun to attract Mrs Benedict who was driving by. There is a much reproduced photograph of Dean standing with his rifle over his shoulders, holding it in a way which gave him a sort of a crucified pose. A subservient Elizabeth Taylor is kneeling at his feet, playing an adoring Mary Magdelena to his Jesus. The shot was not in the film and gives a completely wrong idea of their relationship. Mrs Benedict was never subservient to Jett. He may have been in love with her but there was no indication that she ever more than liked him. A variation of the same still was also reproduced as a crude poster. The rifle was removed and a drooping cigarette was put in Dean's hand near Taylor's mouth.

Jett invited Mrs Benedict into his homely shack. There were pictures of girlies on the wall and a photograph of her in her wedding dress torn out of an old newspaper. There were books on how to improve himself lying around on the table.

Elizabeth Taylor and James Dean in *Giant*

The scene which followed was acted with all of Dean's shy awkwardness, the boyish charm and sexiness coming into gentle play. He entertained her to tea, taking a quick and private shot of whisky to steady his nerves; it was, with hindsight, the first indication that Rink was on the booze.

Jett paid Leslie a pretty compliment and asked if she had a sister back home.

'Money ain't all,' she said.

'Not when you got it,' he replied.

Leslie was impressed by his efforts and wondered why the Mexican Indians hadn't improved themselves as he had done. He was insulted by the comparison, having no wish to

be identified with 'a bunch of wetbacks'. His racism shocked her.

The racism, though it was condemned in the strongest terms throughout the movie, nevertheless, still offended the Mexicans and a number of scenes were cut in Mexico, the authorities fearing there might be attacks on US tourists and Texans in particular.

Jett was 'down to his last collar button' when he finally struck oil, a gushing climax, which had him transfixed, showering in it. Still covered in oil he drove over to the Benedicts (the first time he'd been to the mansion in years) to tell them about his good fortune. They were sitting around in their nice clean clothes on their nice white porch.

'My well came in!' He roared with laughter. 'Everybody thought I had a duster! There ain't nothing you can do about it.' He taunted them, his arms outstretched. Almost balletic in his movements, Rink was both triumphant and threatening. 'I'm rich, Bick. I'm the richest. I'm a rich boy. Me, I'm going to have more money than you ever thought you could have, you and the rest of all you stinking sons of Benedicts.'

All the years of rejection and poverty, the bottled-up anger poured out of him. The performance, highly mannered, very artificial, very stylized, very theatrical, very Method, was a *tour de force*.

Leslie tried to be nice to him. He repaid her kindness by making a pass at her. 'You always did look pretty, pretty good enough to eat.' Bick, furious, took a punch at him and had to be restrained. While he was being held, Jett punched him viciously three times before driving off.

'You should have shot that fellow a long time ago,' said Bick's uncle (Chill Wills.) 'Now he's much too rich to kill.'

Time passed. The transition from likeable scruffy cowhand to monster tycoon was so

Rock Hudson, James Dean
and Elizabeth Taylor in
Giant

abrupt that Dean had no chance to build and develop the bad side of his character. The only evidence of his overstepping the mark was one measly shot of him driving into a car and instead of apologising to the driver, he got out and punched him.

More time passed. Jett Rink got older. On Christmas Day, the year of Pearl Harbor, he arrived at the Benedict mansion to talk a little business. He had come to persuade Bick to turn his cattle ranch into an oilfield; it was an offer the drunk and pathetic Bick could no longer afford to refuse. Jett's triumph over a man he had disliked and envied for so long was complete.

The wardrobe and make-up departments gave Dean all the trappings of middle-age:

hat, coat, white scarf, gloves, pencil-thin moustache. His hair was greyed and shaved to give him a receding hair-line. He wore dark glasses. It was not enough. Taylor and Hudson were far more convincing in middle-age than he ever was. It was Dean's boyish body which gave him away.

Jett invited all Texas to the formal opening of the Jett Rink Airport and Hotel Emperador. His motorcade drove through the main street. He was a tiny and somewhat absurd figure, barely coming up above the rim of the car door. He waved to the Benedicts with his familiar slicing gesture. They were more put out to find that their daughter (also called Luz) was the parade's Beauty Queen.

Jett and Luz (Carroll Baker) sat in an

empty cocktail lounge. Jett, old enough to be her father, attempted to seduce her, proposing after a fashion, but never quite getting round to it. 'Why don't we just announce it tonight?' he suggested. 'Wouldn't that blow the roof off?' The idea amused him; if he couldn't marry the mother he would marry the daughter. It would be the perfect revenge. He had, as usual, been drinking too much.

Shortly afterwards, and now so drunk he could barely walk in a straight line, he entered the reception room to huge applause and the band playing 'The Yellow Rose of Texas'. George Stevens enjoyed himself at the expense of raucous Texans whooping it up; they looked and behaved like stampeding cattle.

Benedict's son, Jordan (Dennis Hopper), had married a Mexican Indian but Jett Rink didn't allow Mexican Indians in his hotel and his wife was humiliated. Determined to avenge the insult, Jordan challenged Jett to a fight. 'Are you the one who married a squaw?' Jett inquired and, while Jordan was being restrained by his bodyguards, he punched him with the same practised vicious aim he had dealt Bick on the porch all those years back.

Bick came to his son's rescue. 'Do you want it here or outside?' They retreated to the wine cellar. A cat made a quick exit. 'You had this coming to you for a long time. Get 'em up.' But Jett was too drunk to get anything up. He cut such a pathetic figure Bick decided he wasn't worth hitting.

Jett re-entered the ballroom and tottered to his seat. Dean looked exactly what Rink was: a vulgar little man, an arrogant pipsqueak. There was a touch of farce about the way he sat, head cocked, half-smiling, half-awake, trying to look sober, listening to Judge Whiteside's ridiculously fulsome introduction. The hypocritical old windbag droned on and on: 'A legend in our time… a great Texan… an outstanding American… a man.' The introduction over, Jett made an attempt to rise. He failed. His head just sank to the table and remained there; it was a Chaplinesque moment.

Dean's final scene was in the empty ballroom. The guests had all left in disgust and only the waiters remained. ('He owns the place, let him enjoy it.') He made his speech to a sea of bare tables: 'Poor Jett… pretty Leslie… give bride… rich Mrs Benedict… she's beautiful… she's lovely… a woman a man wants… a woman a man's got to have…' But it wasn't Dean's voice. He was dead, killed in a crash on the highway a fortnight after he had finished the film. His voice had been dubbed by Nick Adams.

Hands outstretched, looking like a scarecrow, Rink finally collapsed, he and the long table going right over the top in a spectacular and melodramatic crash.

66 He had the ability to take a scene and break it down; sometimes he broke it down into so many bits and pieces that I couldn't see the scene for the trees, so to speak. I must admit that I sometimes underestimated him, and sometimes he overestimated the effects he thought he was getting. Then he might change his approach, do it quick, and if that didn't work we'd effect a compromise. All in all, it was a hell of a headache to work with him. He was always pulling and hauling, and he had developed this cultivated, designed irresponsibility. It's tough on you, he'd seem to imply, but I've just got to do it this way. From the director's point of view that isn't the most delightful sort of fellow to work with. Anyway, he delivered his performance, and he cracked himself up, and I can't say I'm happy about all that's happening about it. There are some people involved in it who don't show up too well.

George Stevens quoted by Hollis Alpert *Saturday Review*

" He takes all that film and shoots every scene from every possible angle – all round the scene, up, down, here and there – and when it's through he gets himself the best editor in town. They then spend a year, sometimes more, selecting from miles and miles of film the best shots and the best scene.

James Dean quoted by Richard Whitehall
Films and Filming

" While he was playing Jett Rink, he was inseparable from Jett Rink; he did NOT become Jett Rink, but Jett Rink was his constant companion.

Mercedes McCambridge *The Quality of Mercy*

" He was original. Impish, compelling, magnetic, utterly winning one moment, obnoxious the next. Definitely gifted. Frequently maddening.

Edna Ferber *A Kind of Magic*

" I didn't like him particularly. He and I and Chill Willis lived in a rented house together for three months while we were doing *Giant* in Texas, and although we each went more or less our own way, Dean was hard to be round. He hated George Stevens, didn't think he was a good director, and he was always angry and full of contempt. He never smiled. He was sulky, and he had no manners. I'm not that concerned with manners – I'll take them where I find them – but Dean didn't have 'em. And he was rough to do a scene with for reasons that only an actor can appreciate. While doing a scene, in the giving and taking, he was just a taker. He would suck everything out and never give back.

Rock Hudson quoted by Ray Loynd *Hollywood Reporter*

" This film clearly shows for the first (and fatefully last time) what his admirers always said he had: a streak of genius. He has caught the Texas accent to nasal perfection, and has mastered the lock-hipped, high-heeled stagger of the wrangler, and the wry little jerks and smirks, tics and switches, grunts and giggles that make up most of the language of the man who talks to himself a good deal more than he does to anyone else.

Time

" As for James Dean, there is no doubt that his death has added poignancy to his every appearance. But there is nothing macabre about it, he is too vital; it is easy to see why the fact of his passing is so hard to accept by so many. Stevens has directed him beautifully, taking full advantage of Dean's unusual ability to act with his whole body as much as with his voice and face.

James Powers *Hollywood Reporter*

" In the light of the current death cult starring the late James Dean it's probably safe to assume that he will be the strongest draw on the *Giant* marquee. No one should be disappointed, and the film only proves what a promising talent has been lost. As the shiftless, envious, bitter ranchhand who hates society, Dean delivers an outstanding portrayal... It's a sock performance.

Hift *Variety*

" Mr Dean plays this curious villain with a stylized spookiness – a sly sort of off-beat languor and slur of language – that concentrates spite. This is a haunting capstone to the brief career of Mr Dean.

Bosley Crowther *New York Times*

" It is James Dean who gives the most striking performance and creates in Jett Rink the most memorable character in *Giant*. Devotees of the cult which has grown up around him since he was killed in an auto

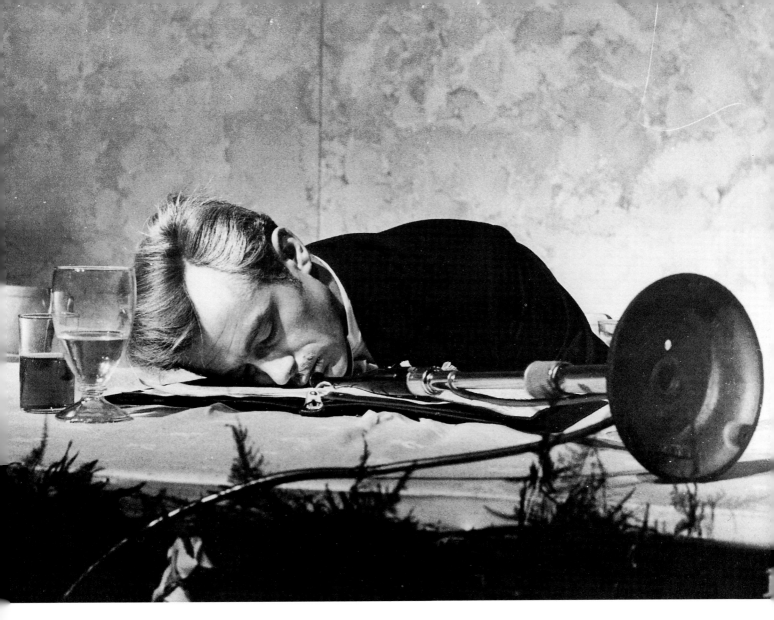

James Dean in *Giant*

crash just after *Giant* was filmed may be somewhat surprised to see him slouching around in dark glasses and a pencil-thin mustache as the dissipated hotel and oil tycoon in the latter stages of the film. But his earlier depiction of the amoral, reckless, animal-like young ranch hand will not only excite his admirers into frenzy, it will make the most sedate onlooker understand why a James Dean cult ever came into existence.

Herbert Kupferberg *New York Herald Tribune*

❝ Much has been written and overwritten about Dean. His acting seemed often a St Vitus dance of pathos, and after a time the mannerisms could become irritating. In *Giant*

he has to pass from crazy mixed-up yokel boy to crazy mixed-up oil tycoon. If he were alive today we would be hoping that he might now shed some of his mannerisms. As it is we can only repeat that this was one of the very few genuine personalities to come up since the war.

Fred Majdalany *Daily Mail*

❝ I found Dean so mannered and exhibitionistic as to be repellent in a way not, perhaps, intended by the role. It is a calculated, erratic and unsubtle performance lacking the depth of his promising work in *East of Eden* under Kazan.

Paul Rotha *Films and Filming*

111

James Dean and George Stevens on the set of *Giant*

❝ As a middle-aged, power-crazed megalomaniac, his limitations are seriously revealed. Looking like a small-time watch salesman, his inarticulateness maddeningly reduces the character to an unintelligible throttle of grunts and nods that arouses neither sympathy nor repugnance. It is a pity James Dean died before he had learned to correct the mistakes he made in *Giant*.

Milton Shulman *Sunday Express*

❝ Mr Dean, with his realistic gulps, hesitations and strangled tardiloquence is ill-suited to the sort of 'literary' dialogue which calls for articulate declamation rather than a manneristic mumble.

Paul Dehn *News Chronicle*

❝ His style of acting is the very antithesis of the sober, well-controlled acting of the other actors in the film.

Louis Marcorelles *Cahiers du cinéma*

❝ James Dean more than fulfils his early promise. Small and cocky, writhing with self-consciousness, with guile, with the pangs of poverty, ignorance, social ineptitude, the quintessence of everything youthful, impossible, impressionable, frustrated and gauche – and yet a 'personality', someone that matters beyond his pathetic present – his performance in the first half of the film (later he is asked to grow old, and cannot manage it) would make *Giant* worth sitting through if it were five hours long.

Isabel Quigly *Spectator*

❝ The acting is moderately adequate by Rock Hudson, good by Elizabeth Taylor, and virtuoso by James Dean whose Jett Rink is a wilful and brilliant variation on the character he made his own, and died for – the baffled, tender, violent adolescent, rejected by the world he rejects. The middle-aged Jett Rink he could not manage: a matured, hopelessly corrupt character was beyond him.

Lindsay Anderson *New Statesman and Nation*

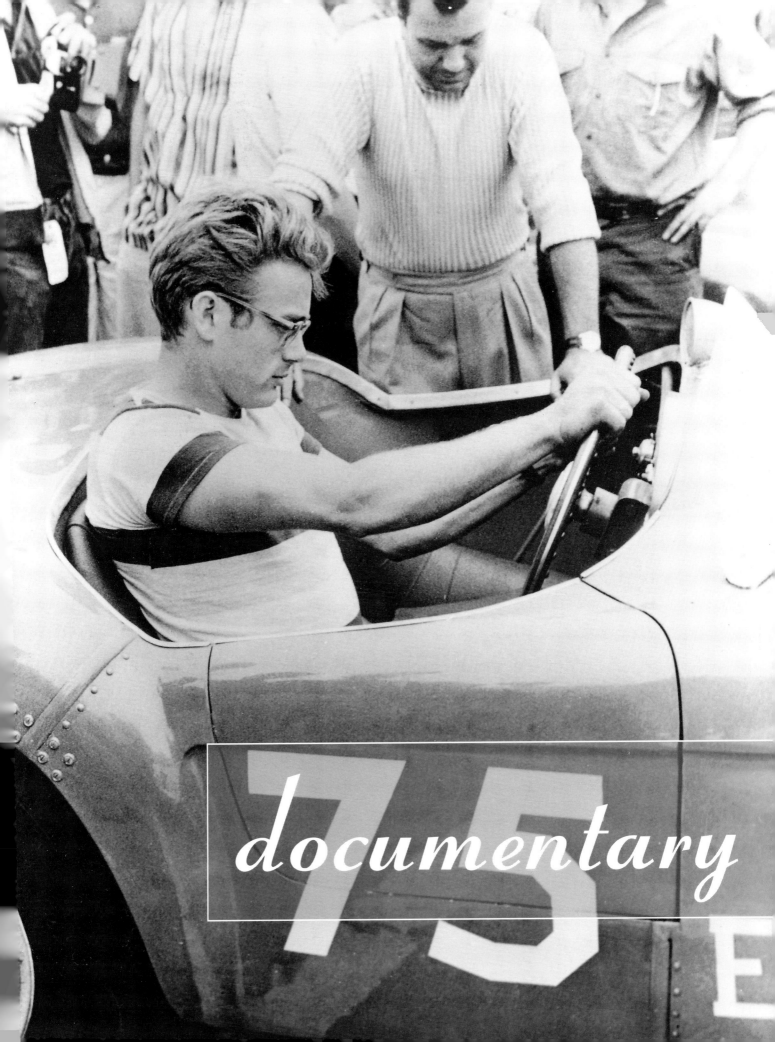

documentary

The Steve Allen Show

Network   NBC
Date   14 October 1956

Steve Allen, top-ranking television and radio personality, paid a special tribute to James Dean one year after his death. 'The Dean legend is without parallel in the experience of our society,' he began. 'A certain segment mourns Dean as they would a departed national hero.'

He then went on to describe Dean as a representative of today's youth: the all-American boy, sensitive, rebellious, filled with a sense of humour, confused, shy, insecure, and yet confident in his power. He quoted actress Mercedes McCambridge, his co-star in *Giant*, as saying that Dean knew more about acting than any other actor she had met.

Allen toured Fairmount, Dean's home town, visiting his high school, and speaking with his grandparents and teenagers, none of whom had anything of interest to say.

Easily the most arresting part of the programme was a tantalizingly brief yet powerful extract from Dean's 1953 television drama, *Life Sentence*, in which he had played a convict harassing a woman on a porch, his mood alternating alarmingly between gentleness and intimidation.

To bring out Dean's Quaker and farming upbringing, a clip was used from another television play, *Harvest*, in which he had played a Quaker farm boy. Since there was no indication on the screen that viewers were watching a TV clip, some audiences would undoubtedly have thought they were seeing genuine footage from his life.

The James Dean Story

Director	Robert Altman
Studio	Warner Bros
Date	13 August 1957
Producer	G. W. George
Screenplay	Stewart Stern
Score	Leith Stevenson
Narrator	Martin Gabel

PARTICIPANTS

The People in Fairmount

His uncle,	Marcus Winslow
His aunt,	Ortense Winslow
His cousin,	Markie Winslow
His grandfather,	Grandpa Dean
His grandmother,	Grandma Dean
His drama teacher,	Adeline Nall
The Nurseryman,	Bing Traster
Owner of the motorcycle shop,	Mr Carter

The People in New York

Owner of Jerry's Bar,	Jerry Luce
Waiter at Jerry's Bar,	Louie de Liso
Taxicab driver,	Arnie Langer
The girl in the apartment,	Arline Sas
The girl at the Actors Studio,	Chris White
The theatrical press agent,	George Ross

The People in California

President of Sigma Nu,	Robert Jewett
Dean's fraternity brother,	John Kalin
Dean's best friend,	Lew Bracker
Actor who shared Dean's apartment,	Glenn Kramer
Owner of the Villa Capri,	Patsy D'Amore
His partner,	Billy Karen
The actress Dean dated,	Lilli Kardell
The California Highway Patrolman,	Officer Nelson

The James Dean Story opened with a car zooming along the highway until it crashed. Many critics found the film tasteless, even ghoulish, and dismissed it, out of hand, as a cheap, tawdry documentary feeding only morbid appetites.

Robert Altman revisited Fairmount (where Dean was brought up), the University of

California (where he studied drama), and his old haunts in New York and Hollywood. There were formal interviews with family, teacher, favourite waiter, taxi-driver, actresses, girlfriends, university contemporaries and room-mates. The interviewer Martin Gabel, who remained off-screen, adopted a manner so formal as to be off-putting.

Grandma showed old snapshots. Drama teacher Adeline Nall produced an orchid schoolboy Dean had painted for her. Friend Lew Bracker opened a box of personal belongings Dean had left with him just before his fatal crash. The box contained fan mail, phone numbers on scraps of paper, bills, bank statements, a letter from his laundry and a newspaper clipping about one of his races. More interestingly, Bracker said that Dean had wanted to become a director because 'there was more freedom of movement in direction than acting.'

Actress Christine White remembered how they had worked for two months on their audition piece for The Actors Studio and how he had never played the scene the same way twice, even on the day of the audition.

Taxi-driver Arnie Lager recalled how Dean was always studying people, taking their physical characteristics and using it in his acting. 'He used objects beautifully. He had a way of diverting attention from other people.'

Nicholas Ray, who did not appear, was quoted as saying that 'Jimmy belonged to a private club which had only a few members.'

The best things about the documentary were the stills and photographs, especially those by Denis Stock and Roy Schatt taken in New York and Fairmount. The worst thing was Stewart Stern's wordy and pretentious commentary: "He seemed to express some of the things they [Dean's fans] couldn't find the words for: rage, rebellion, hope, the lonely awareness that growing up is pain… a hero

made of their loneliness, a legend woven from their restlessness, their energy, their despair".

Martin Gabel's ponderous and pompous delivery would have been excessive at a State Funeral. But there was worse to come:

"He took his envy to the beach. He looked at the ocean (shot of ocean) and he was jealous of its power. He envied the gulls for having found each other. He envied them their freedom and their solitary flights (shot of solitary gull). Suddenly he knew that as an actor he could be the ocean and flood everything with his power (waves flooded the screen). As an actor he could be a gull and rise higher than any living thing. He would become an actor, really an actor, he would conquer New York and press the theatre to his feet. Then he would come back and conquer Hollywood. He would rise so high, he would almost vanish and everyone would beg him to come back, and he saw a dead bird in the sand (shot of dead bird) and wept for it. But he was on his way (shot of footprints in the sand), Jimmy Dean was going to be somebody".

In Fairmount there were pictures of the town, his home, the surrounding farmland, the Quaker church where he prayed and his high school. There were shots of a lonely tree, his mother's grave and a poem he had sent to the local newspaper. There was also a tape-recording he had made of his grandfather and examples of his art work and sculpture, including a tiny faceless statue which he had called Self.

In New York Dean lived in a one-room apartment which he shared with musician Leonard Rosenman and which he had described as 'a wastepaper basket with walls', the only witty remark in the whole film.

The script dealt only in banalities. Audiences learned that Dean's 'appetites were large but he was never quite full, neither was his suitcase… Afraid of his solitariness and his dreams, he prowled the night like a hunter.' Earlier they had learned that as a boy he had 'liked animals because they accepted him as he was and they were gentle'.

Stern quoted from William K. Zinsser's review of *East of Eden*, which had appeared in *The New York Herald Tribune*, feeling that Zinsser had described not just Cal Trask but Jimmy Dean as well: "Everything about him suggests the lonely misunderstood nineteen-year-old. He has the wounded look of an orphan trying to piece together the shabby facts of his heritage. Occasionally he smiles as if at some dark joke known only to himself. You sense badness in him but you also like him".

Later, when Dean was quoted talking about his mother, it seemed as if Jimmy Dean was quoting John Steinbeck: 'She wouldn't have died on me if I hadn't been bad. She would have loved me and taken care of me. If you couldn't love me nobody can. I have been bad all my life so I've never deserved anything good.'

Apart from the interviews, Altman's documentary also included the road safety commercial Dean had made just before he died and newsreel footage from the *Giant* premiere. Best of all, there was the deeply moving screen test he made for *East of Eden*, which had never been shown before.

Dean (Cal) and Richard Davalos (Aron) were discovered in their bedroom. Dean, nearest to the camera, was deep in shadow.

Cal: You're the one that dad loves. He doesn't love me. Never has. This is my son, Aron that is, thinks I got a great idea here. This mother-son Cal, who saved his money when we were kids and bought him a beautiful jack-knife

and you got him a lousy, mangy, little old dog you'd picked up somewhere. (*The voice cracks.*) Well, he loved that dog, Aron. He didn't even say thank you for my jack-knife. Didn't say nothing. (*He picks up his recorder and starts to play.*)

Aron: What have you ever done to deserve dad's love? What I mean is. Like who tried to be decent to him and make things half way pleasant?

Cal: (*Looking up at him from under his eyelashes, the classic Dean look*) You did.

Aron: And what have you done? Ever since I can remember you've growled at him and snapped at him. You can't win anybody's love by fighting them every minute, Cal. You've got to fight with them. You've got to show them you're on their side. Cal, Why don't you give dad a chance? Why don't you show him you love him?

Cal: HOW? (*The inner pain is acute.*)

Aron: It's so easy. Just tell him. Show him. Why don't you do something for him. It's so easy. You'll see it's the simplest thing in the world

Cal: (*Nodding in agreement*) I know it. I know it is, Aron.

The camera was on Dean practically all the time, his eyes red-rimmed from crying, ringed with dark circles, the face desolate and hurt. It is a great pity that the scene did not end up in the film.

The scene was shot. There is a still of Aron lying naked in bed, hands under sheets, his head turned towards Cal, waiting, almost yearning, for Cal to come to bed. Cal sits on a chair, half-naked, playing his recorder. The homoeroticism is obvious in the picture and, perhaps, this was one reason why the scene

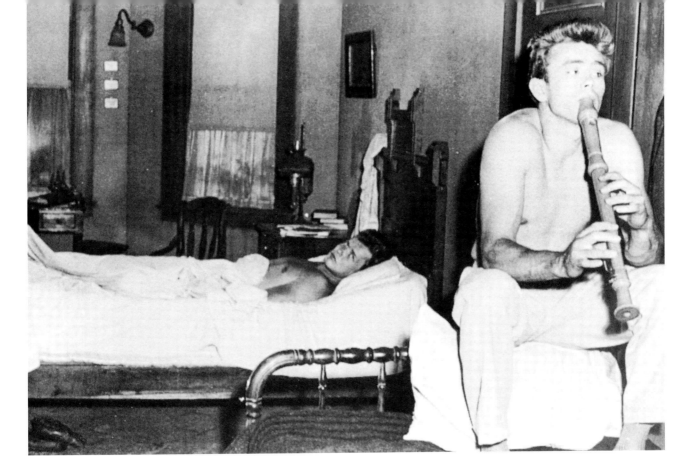

did not appear in the final film. Cal could kill
Aron (that was in the Bible) but in the 1950s,
with the censor still around, any suggestion,
any hint of brotherly incest could not be
countenanced. There was nothing erotic about
the screen test. Dean was fully clothed and
Davelos was in his buttoned-up pajamas.

The James Dean Story ended, as it had
begun, with the car crash plus the inevitable
shot of a dead bird in the sea. There were
photographs of the debris and a highway
patrolman read out his report on the accident.
This was followed by footage of the funeral
cortège (his ex-basketball team acting as
pallbearers), and more squirm-making
verbiage along the lines of: 'He was able to
reach into a dark theatre and let each person
know that they were not alone and to unveil
that single quality which most of us conceal,
that wonderful sense of our own inexpressible
sweetness.'

All that remained then was for a glib bit of
psychiatry ('We can say he despised the thing
he was and loved the thing he was trying to

become') and for Tommy Sands to sing 'Let
Me Be Loved', a maudlin song by James
Livingston and Ray Evans.

❝ Undoubtedly the Dean aficionados will
not be in the mood to carp about the way
their hero has been canonized. They'll love it,
and should buy thousands of tickets to show
their appreciation. The less enchanted, which
will include many of those who respected
Dean's ability, may be amused, bewildered,
irritated and/or frightened by the way the film
so reverently raises to near sainthood a symbol
of inarticulate rebellion.

Vincent Canby *Motion Picture Herald*

❝ I found it a sly, silly, inaccurate, tasteless,
and finally repellent film. It is sordid in
intention and inept in execution. I hope
people will NOT go to see it in large numbers.

Anthony Carthew *Daily Herald*

❝ No bodysnatchers should miss this.

Sunday Graphic

James Dean – The First American Teenager

Alternative title:
Idol – The Story of James Dean

Director	Ray Connolly
Company	Visual Programme Systems
Date	1976
Producers	David Puttnam
	Sandy Lieberson
Screenplay	Ray Connolly
Commentary	Ray Connolly
Narrator	Stacy Keach
Photography	Peter Hannan, Mike Molloy,
	Robert Gersicoff
Editor	Peter Hollywood
Music/songs	Elton John, David Bowie, The Eagles

66 There's one wonderful thing about dead movie stars. They can't disappoint you. That's all the live ones are capable of doing.

Kenneth Kendall, sculptor and artist

Sal Mineo and James Dean in *Rebel Without a Cause*

James Dean – The First American Teenager, made 20 years after his death, was full of memorable and haunting classic images of Dean. There were interviews with colleagues and friends, clips from his three major films and clips from four unnamed television plays. There was also newsreel footage of him motor-car racing (his major obsession apart from acting) and the commercial for road safety he had made a few days before he died on the highway.

'There is nothing nostalgic about James Dean,' narrated Stacy Keach in a voice-over. 'He remains a contemporary hero, an image as relevant today as it was 20 years ago.'

The opening pre-credit sequence used a collage of stills and dialogue from his films to make it seem as if Dean were talking about himself 'My mother, she's not dead and gone to heaven, has she?… I've got to know who I

am, what I'm like… Talk to me, father…
You're tearing me apart!… Talk to me,
please…'

There were tantalizingly brief extracts from
his television plays: *A Long Time Till Dawn*
(screaming at the police from a window before
being gunned down); *Life Sentence* (as a
convict on a porch chatting up a woman,
mixing charm and menace); *The Unlighted
Road* (saying goodbye to his girlfriend before
going off to hand himself in to the police);
and a religious drama, *Hill Number One*, his
earliest professional work, unexpectedly cast
as John the Apostle.

Also included was his screen test for *East of
Eden*. Director Elia Kazan was quoted as
saying that Jimmy was Cal. 'He had a grudge
against all fathers. He was vengeful, he had a
sense of a lowness and of being persecuted
and he was suspicious.'

Sal Mineo, who had played Plato in *Rebel
Without a Cause*, claimed that Dean had
started the entire youth movement and that he
was the first actor to give teenagers an
identification of any kind. 'Before Jimmy
Dean you were either a baby or you were a
man. In between was just sort of one of those
terrible stages you had to get out of terribly
quickly and he didn't. He gave the teenager a
status.'

Nicholas Ray, director of *Rebel Without a
Cause*, said that at the time he thought Dean's
talent would have surpassed everybody,
Marlon Brando, Toshiro Mifune, Gerard
Philipe and Laurence Olivier. Later he had
changed his mind only in respect of Olivier.

Carroll Baker, sitting by a fireside, all
dressed up (to go where?), remembered her
first day in front of the cameras on *Giant*
which she described as 'a fair competition
between two New York Studio Actors
upstaging each other', until he suddenly
grabbed her under the table: 'I went into utter

shock,' she told viewers, 'and I thought that
was a really very dirty thing to do because I
think he did it in order to try and throw me in
the scene.'

Former room-mate and musician Leonard
Rosenman, who had written the theme music
for *East of Eden* and *Rebel Without a Cause*
and taught Dean the piano, was filmed
walking by a sea-shore. He thought that Dean
had identified with his roles because he had
no real identity. He remembered what a
painful experience reading had been for him
and how he had got into the correct frame of
mind for the cliff-top scene in *Rebel* with the
help of a blood-soaked apple.

Singer Sammy Davis Jr recalled that he had
invited Dean to a party so that he could meet
Marlon Brando. Dean arrived, dressed in the
sort of gear Brando had worn in *The Wild
One*. Brando arrived in a suit and was not
amused. Christine White also spoke of Dean's
fixation with Brando. She was coy about
whether she had had an affair with him or
not, while leaving the impression that she had.

White also remembered how she and Dean
had rehearsed for the Actors Studio audition
'for two tedious months in taxi cabs, in
Central Park, in my apartment, on the roof,
along the street, in restaurants. Wherever we
were, we rehearsed. We'd say to the taxi
driver: hey, want to see a scene?'

Gene Owen, his drama teacher at
university, and her husband talked about
Dean's affection for Pier Angeli. So did
Vampira, star of the Ed Wood horror movies.
Some people thought he was bisexual.
Nicholas Ray said Dean was normal. 'What in
the hell is normal?' he roared, his eyepatch
and shock of unruly white hair making him
look perfect casting for an Ed Wood movie.

Actress Leslie Caron recalled Dean's smile,
his graceful movements of head and body, his
charm, his voice. Actor John Larson thought

Dean was a fake and said that he personally 'didn't buy Dean's hurt little looks'.

Kenneth Kendall, who had made a bust and many drawings of Dean, displayed some of the memorabilia he had collected over the years: two ties and the suit Dean had worn in the scene on the Ferris wheel in *East of Eden*, a pair of levis from *Rebel Without a Cause*, and a cummerbund and stand-up collar from *Giant*.

Others who appeared were Corey Allen (who played Buzz, the gang leader, in *Rebel Without a Cause*), Captain E. Tripke of the California Highway Patrol (who had been at the scene of the fatal car crash), agent Peter Witt, and actor Dennis Hopper.

The 17-year-old Hopper had worked with Dean in *Rebel Without a Cause* and later *Giant*. He was filmed in the middle of the desert, driving up in his truck and wearing a cowboy hat. He said that Dean was magic and that, as a drama teacher, Dean had affected him as much as Lee Strasberg had done at The Actors Studio. He remembered how they had smoked grass together. He also recalled that Dean had been so nervous about acting with Elizabeth Taylor in *Giant* that he had been barely able to speak before their first scene together. He found an original way of getting over his nerves. He urinated in front of the whole company.

Hopper also recalled how much Dean had admired Marlon Brando and Montgomery Clift and how he had said that the reason he was going to make it was because 'I've got Marlon Brando in this hand saying, 'Screw you!' and I've got Montgomery Clift in this hand saying, 'Help me!' And somewhere in between these two actors was James Dean.'

" What continues to amaze, as a lingering impression, is how little the Dean material – and indeed the image – has aged.

Hawk *Variety*

" Personally, I find all those bruised-eyes, up-from-under looks of Dean's embarrassingly reminiscent of childhood tactics: the attempt to get Daddy to apologise for the latest clobberings. But then I have a well-developed aversion to actors who use their art as conscious therapy – which I have a feeling Dean is doing endlessly.

Russell Davies *Observer*

" As somebody still under Dean's spell (who went to *Rebel* prepared to sneer at a poor man's Brando and left the cinema intoxicated by a new kind of acting) it's hard to say whether the film has got far in explaining The Young Master's magic.

Shaun Usher *Daily Mail*

" Connolly's own commentary, narrated in awed tones by Stacy Keach, blankets the portrait in shallow observations, leaving the spectator without any intelligent explanation of Dean's contemporary and continuing appeal.

Geoff Brown *Monthly Film Bulletin*

" These patchwork sequences from Dean's three movies and interviews make no case for his relevance then or now… If anything, the film excerpts from *East of Eden*, *Rebel Without a Cause* and *Giant* leave one to wonder what the fuss was about. The aura has left the image and only the pout remains. The interviews amount to a number of people saying that actually they didn't know him all that well.

Richard Eder *New York Times*

" Hollywood may bury its heroes. But the cash register lives on and on.

James Murray *Daily Express*

121

Hollywood:
I Rebelli 'James Dean'

English title:
Hollywood: The Rebels 'James Dean'

Director	Claudio Masenza
Studio	Clak
Date	1982
Producer	Donatella Baglivo
Music	Flavio Emilio Scogna
Photography	Giancarlo Formichi

PARTICIPANTS

Corey Allen,	actor
William Bast,	friend and biographer
Ruth Goetz,	playwright
Bill Gunn,	actor and friend
Julie Harris,	actress
Venable Herndon,	biographer
Dennis Hopper,	actor and director
Tab Hunter,	actor
Martin Landau,	actor
Adeline Nall,	teacher
Leonard Rosenman,	music composer
Beulah Roth,	friend
Roy Schatt,	photographer
Dizzy Sheridan,	dancer
Stewart Stern,	writer
Bob Thomas,	biographer
Christine White,	actress
Ortense Winslow,	aunt

Hollywood: The Rebels were three quite separate documentaries on Marlon Brando, Montgomery Clift and James Dean.

The James Dean documentary opened with a pre-credit sequence of Dean being shot at an open window in an unidentified scene from one of his television plays. It was in fact from *A Long Time Till Dawn* by Rod Serling, Dean's first major television role.

There were brief extracts from some of his other television work: as Apostle John addressing Jesus's disciples in *Hill Number 1*, as a convict threatening a woman ('I'll break

Marlon Brando visits Elia Kazan, Julie Harris and James Dean during the shooting of East of Eden

your skull!') in *Life Sentence*, and as a motorist being fired at by a man in a pursuing car in *The Unlighted Road*.

There was also his screen test for *East of Eden* (deeply moving no matter how many times it is seen), his commercials for Pepsi and road safety, and a good selection of stills, portraits and family snap shots.

The first person to be interviewed was actor Martin Landau, who had met Dean at one of television's open casting calls in the early 1950s, the Golden Age of television, which gave so many young New York actors their first chance. They used to read Shakespeare and listen to music together. He said that Dean really had represented the Fifties more than any single person: 'He was the fellow who all teenagers of this country and all of the young people in their twenties said, Yes, that's how I felt. Yes, that's me, I understand that person… We always watched grows-ups in movies. We had never really seen a true portrayal or a representation of the turmoil that was being felt by most young people.'

Ortense Winslow, Dean's aunt who had brought him up when his mother died, sat in a rocking chair and described him as a cute, pretty little boy ('I've heard people say, too pretty to be a boy') and she remembered how 'he loved acting more than anything else.' When Dean had first appeared on television, the family had bought a TV set. The thing that had impressed her the most was how thin he had looked. 'I guess,' she observed, 'he wasn't eating like usual.'

Adeline Nall, his drama schoolteacher at Fairmount High School, was observed standing at a lectern, addressing an empty classroom.

Actress Julie Harris, who described him as mercurial, unpredictable and very beguiling, said he was a wonderful, inventive actor who

123

James Dean auditions
for *East of Eden*

always came to every scene fresh. She remembered the last day of shooting *East of Eden* and how she had found him in his caravan, 'sobbing like a lost little boy, vulnerable, very sweet'.

Stewart Stern, who wrote the screenplay for *Rebel Without a Cause*, sat by his swimming pool and said Dean had brought a poetic reality to the screen he had never seen before. He recalled how they had made animal noises at their first meeting (mooing, grunting, bleating) and how later when Dean had worked for Warner Bros, Dean had gone around changing the names on the doors so that people wanting to see Jack Warner would find themselves facing a row of urinals and those wanting the men's room would find themselves in Warner's office.

Biographer William Bast sat by his swimming pool and remembered how they had met at the University of California when they were both on the Theatre Arts programme. Dean had been moody, surly, sulky and he had a frightening volatile temper. He could go for three days without speaking ('very unnerving to live with') and then he would be warm and outgoing ('the best friend you ever had'). He recalled his performance in *Macbeth*: 'the most dreadful Indiana accent, this terrible farmboy twang, couldn't pronounce the Shakespeare, couldn't get his tongue round it, the worst actor I've seen.'

Bast couldn't resist an innuendo: 'It was his philosophy that an actor had to do everything, had to experiment with everything, which certainly gave him license to do anything he wanted to do.'

Musician Leonard Rosenman, friend, mentor and 'sort of father figure', sat by his swimming pool and remembered how he had been in on the production of *East of Eden* right from the beginning and how he had written the music before the scenes were being shot and had played the music to the actors before they acted. In those areas where the music rather than the dialogue carried the scene, he had co-directed with Kazan.

Actress Christine White (who described Dean as 'a funny little boy') remembered how when they were rehearsing their audition piece for The Actors Studio they would show it to anybody who would watch: taxi-drivers, bartenders, jewellery store assistants.

Dancer Dizzy Sheridan, recalled their first meeting when he had taken out his two front teeth and dropped them in his drink and how amused she had been. They had lived together in a dingy hotel and she used to wash his socks and underwear. They would hug, kiss, make love and sleep in the same bed and though she did not want to go into intimate details, she admitted they 'did what people in love do'. Once Dean's career had taken off, however, the affair had ended.

Actor Dennis Hopper, in his cowboy hat, sat in the shrubbery and remembered what Dean had said to him: 'You know what's going to make me famous: I've got Brando in this hand saying, 'Fuck You! I've got Montgomery Clift in this hand saying, 'Please forgive me.' (When he had told the story in *James Dean – The First American Teenager* back 1976 it had been 'Help me!') Clift had to keep changing his telephone number because Dean constantly pestered him.

Hopper had asked Dean about acting. His advice had been to stop acting: 'Don't show it, just do it. Don't act smoking a cigarette, smoke a cigarette.' He repeated his story of Dean urinating in front of everybody on the set of *Giant*.

Actor Corey Allen sat among the shrubbery in his own home (the television on

beside him) and recalled a moment when Dean had brought him a cup of water on the set of *Rebel Without a Cause*, which was a cue for the music on the soundtrack to get all sentimental.

Photographer Roy Schatt remembered Dean sitting in a chair in the middle of the road smoking a cigarette and holding up the traffic. Schatt also remembered Dean spending a whole week making a home movie, but he had never seen any of it and didn't know what had become of it.

Playwright Ruth Goetz gave a vivid picture of Dean arriving to audition for *The Immoralist*, the play she and her husband, Augustus, had based on André Gide's novel. Dean came in wearing a large ten gallon hat, cowboy boots, bright green vest, a very posh English sports jacket with leather patches on the elbow, and blue jeans, unusual and unlikely clothes to be wearing to an audition for an Arab street boy. But the moment he had begun to read she thought he was marvellous. 'He was instinctually [sic], absolutely right. He had the quality of sweetness and charming attractiveness and at the same time a nasty undercurrent of suggestiveness and sexuality.'

His abominable behaviour at rehearsal hadn't pleased anybody: he didn't work, he couldn't learn his lines, he was slovenly and late. 'He was the most exasperating actor I ever worked with', said Goetz. However, came the first night of the try-out in Philadelphia, he was transformed. On stage he was thoroughly professional; it was only backstage that he was detestable and horrid. Two nights after they had opened in New York he gave in his notice and 'he didn't give a damn.'

Forever James Dean

Director	Ara Chekmayan
Studio	Warner Bros
Release	1988
Producer	Ara Chekmayan
Associate	Christine Cameron
Executive producers	Jeff Lawenda, Michael Yudin
Screenplay	Ara Chekmayan
Research	Susan Bluttman, David Loehr
Photographer	Chuck Levey

Forever James Dean opened with a number of classic photographs and Chris Buson singing George Elworth's 'American Rebel' ('Rebel James Dean, somewhere between a boy and a man'). The narrator began by reminding viewers that in a career lasting 30 years, Clark Gable had made 67 pictures, that Humphrey Bogart in 27 years had made 80 pictures, and that Gary Cooper in 35 years had made 92 pictures. James Dean, in a career which lasted 16 months, had made 3 pictures.

Dean was described as a complex person on and off-screen, an introvert and exhibitionist, polite and rude, a loner and a charmer, who played with his congas. No one, said the narrator, had ever captured the feelings of being young in all its insecurities, confusions and loneliness better than Dean had. 'He expressed the anguish of growing up as nobody had done before.' This statement was backed up by the inevitable clip from *Rebel Without a Cause* of Dean screaming, 'YOU'RE TEARING ME APART!'

There were extracts from his three major films, a very brief glimpse of him in a Pepsi commercial, and also a clip of the bizarre and stupid things people were prepared to do on the popular game show, *Beat the Clock*, for which he had been a backstage stunt-tester.

There was newsreel footage of Italian actress Pier Angeli (described as 'the love of his life') getting married to singer Vic Damone

and footage from the annual three-day celebrations held on the anniversary of his death in Fairmount, Dean's hometown. The event includes a street fair, an antique car parade and a James Dean lookalike competition.

There were interviews with actors, friends and acquaintances. Julie Harris, who acted with him in *East of Eden*, likened him to a comet and to Tom Sawyer. Fairmount High School drama teacher Adeline Nall said of his performance as Cal Trask in *East of Eden*, 'That's my boy up there. I could just reach up there and touch him. He was Jimmy Dean, the kid I knew. Beautifully done.'

William Bast, his friend and biographer (who described Dean as uncommunicative and surly) said that Cal Trask was a role created for him. 'The story embodied his relationship

with his father; it utilized his loneliness, his isolation from the rest of the world, the perversity of his perspective, his humour, his need for love.'

Five of the actors who had played the gang in *Rebel Without a Cause* – Jack Grinnage, Frank Mazolla, Beverly Long, Steffi Sidney and Corey Allen – were interviewed in front of a car on the very spot where the gang had taunted Jim Stark (Dean's role) in the film. Corey, who had played Buzz, the gang leader whose car went over the cliff, said he didn't feel Dean as an actor was portraying his vulnerability so much as sharing his vulnerability.

Thirty years on everybody was in their 50s and looked it; and this was especially true of the kids he had gone to school with in Fairmount. One of them remembered his

performance as Frankenstein's monster ('real scary'). Another declared categorically that Dean was not homosexual and that, though he was not prepared to go into details, he had proof.

Artist and sculptor Kenneth Kendall, who has made numerous oil paintings and a bronze bust of Dean, said that Dean's acting was nothing like Marlon Brando's acting: 'Marlon is heavy as lead compared to Jimmy. Jimmy is mercurial and light and dancing all over the place. That's not Marlon at all.'

Kendall then went on to make an interesting point: 'We lost two actors in that crash. James Dean and Marlon Brando, because if James Dean had been alive, Marlon couldn't let Jimmy walk the town away from him. We would have seen a lot more out of Brando than we have.'

James Dean in
Rebel Without a Cause

Bye Bye Jimmy

Director	Paul Watson
Company	Lonewolf
Date	1990
Producer	Nick Taylor
Cameraman	John Metcalfe
Narrator	Rick Clemente

Bye Bye Jimmy opened with 'the chicken run' from *Rebel Without a Cause*. Buzz (Alan Corey), the gang leader, was leaning out of his car window, explained to Jim Stark (James Dean) what they had to do. 'Hey, Toreador, she signals and we head for the edge and the first man who jumps is a chicken. All right?' A few minutes later Buzz plunged into the sea and was dead.

On 30 September 1955 Dean left Hollywood in his new Porsche Spyder with his mechanic, Roly Witherich, to race at Salinas in California. Just outside Bakersfield at The Grapevine, a roadside cafe, he received a speeding ticket. He made one more stop at Blackwell's Corner for a Coke and an apple. At 5.45 p.m. he collided with another car at the junction of Highways 41 and 466. His last words were: 'That guy's got to stop, he'll see us.' But Donald Turnupseed, the driver of the other car, never saw them.

On 30th September each year enthusiasts from all over Southern California, many of them not born when Dean died, take part in The Annual James Dean Memorial Cruise, a tribute and homage to 'that maverick loner whose angry young man style they emulate'. Anybody can participate. All they need is a pre-1955 car. 'Not morbid,' insisted one young female fan, 'the only way we can say thanks.'

Bye Bye Jimmy joined the period cars on the road and retraced Dean's last journey accompanied by songs by The Beach Boys, Jerry Lee Lewis and Buddy Holly on the soundtrack. There were photographs, stills,

James Dean and Natalie Wood in *Rebel Without a Cause*

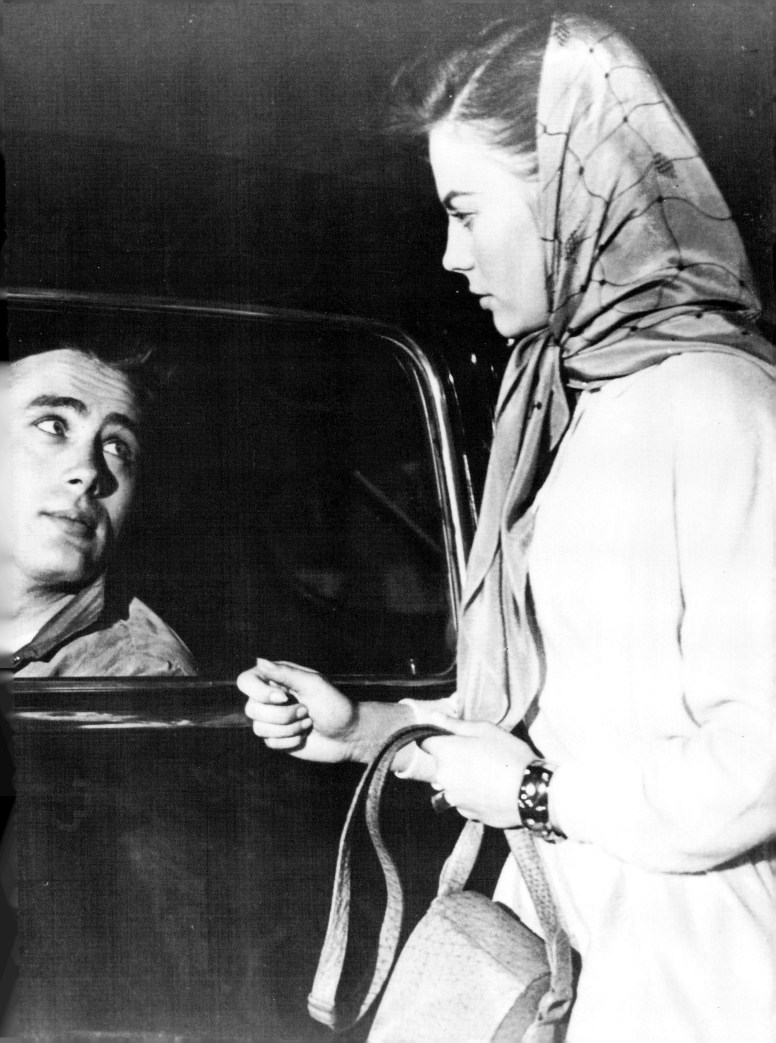

footage from his films, and anecdotes from friends, fans and contemporaries. Actor Corey recollected how many youngsters in the 1950s had thought, erroneously, that in order to be themselves they had to be like Jimmy Dean.

Composer Leonard Rosenman remembered how he had been shocked and not shocked by Dean's death because everybody had seemed to expect something like that would happen. He recalled his and Jo Van Fleet's 'great anger at such a gifted man wasting the most precious thing he had been given by just throwing it away'.

Rosenman also remembered a conversation he had had with Marlon Brando in which Brando had told him that he ought to recommend Dean to go into some kind of therapy because he thought Dean was crazy. (Dean was, in fact, having analysis when he died.)

Brando's arrival on Broadway in 1947 in Tennessee Williams's *A Streetcar Named Desire* and in Elia Kazan's film version of the play in 1951 had spawned a generation of imitators. It seemed to producer Harve Bennet that Dean was 'self-consciously, preeminently, obviously the first imitator'. He recalled the laughter that had greeted Dean's accent when he had played Malcolm in a college production of *Macbeth*. Bennet, who had been at the University of California with him, believed he 'had enormous talent, if no social grace'.

Dick Eschleman, also a classmate at UCLA, reminisced about Dean's dissatisfaction with the fraternity and that he had not wanted to study Law but Theatre Arts, and had finally dropped out. Eschleman also remembered Dean coming off-stage and picking up his spectacles from the prompt corner. 'I don't think I have ever seen such thick lenses.'

Phil Hill, former world racing champion, said Dean had a fair amount of talent as a driver but that he also had 'a scary element' which was unpredictable.

Edward Tripke, the police officer at the scene of the accident and now retired, stood at the intersection near a signpost which read: 'James Dean 1931 February 8 – 1955 September 30 p.m. 5.59'. He recalled Dean's broken neck and tangled feet. There were photographs of the wreckage. The Porsche had later toured the country as part of a road safety campaign. Fans used to tear bits of the metal off for souvenirs. In 1960 the car mysteriously disappeared and it has never been found.

Bye Bye Jimmy ended with the road safety commercial Dean had made just before he died. 'Have you ever been in a drag race?' asked actor Gig Young, his interviewer. A drag race is a race between two cars to determine who can accelerate fastest from a standstill. In the 1950s youngsters were doing this on the public highways at night. There were many accidents, often with cars not taking part in the race!

'Are you kidding me?' replied Dean. 'I am extra cautious. I don't have the urge to speed on the highway.'

James Dean in *Giant*

related works

Screen and Stage Works Relating to James Dean

On screen and stage there have been a number of stories either about James Dean or inspired by James Dean.

The Myth Makers

Television

Series	Play of the Week
Network	Granada
Date	16 April 1958
Writer	William Bast
Director	Silvio Narizzano

Cast

Kate Reid / Pat English
John Sullivan / Colin Douglas
David Nolan / Vera Cook / Peter Madden

William Bast's television drama dealt with the impact of the death of a young celebrity idolized by millions of teenagers. His body was brought back to his home town for burial, accompanied by hysterical fans and a voracious press corps.

The myth makers wanted to orchestrate the event in order to get maximum publicity for the star's last picture. Those who had known the dead man and his true nature, were convinced that the fast-growing cult was not only macabre but dangerous.

To Climb Steep Hills

Television

Series	Straightaway
Network	ABC
Date	28 March 1962
Writer	n/a
Director	n/a

Cast

Paul Carr / Brian Kelly / John Ashley

To Climb Steep Hills concerned a young, car-racing movie star. The character was modelled on Dean and played by Paul Carr.

The Movie Star

Television

Series	DuPont Show of the Month
Network	NBC
Date	10 June 1962
Writer	William Bast
Adaptor	Robert Crean

Cast

Kathleen Widdoes / Dane Clark
Norma Crane / Harry Townes

The Movie Star was an adaptation of William Bast's *The Myth Makers*. Bast felt the change of title and the adaptation's more explicit identification with Dean had undermined the whole concept of the play he had originally written.

Badlands

Film

Director	Terrence Malick
Studio	Warner Bros
Release	1974
Writer	Terrence Malick
Producer	Terrence Malick
Photography	Brian Probyn, Tak Fujimoto, Stevan Larner
Music	George Tipton

Role	Cast
Kit	Martin Sheen
Holly	Sissy Spacek
Father	Warren Oates
Cato	Ramon Bieri
Deputy	Alan Vint
Sheriff	Gary Littlejohn
Rich Man	John Cater
Boy	Bryan Montgomery
Girl	Gail Threikeld
Clerk	Charles Fitzpatrick

❝ You know what this son of a bitch looks like. You know, don't you? I'd kiss your arse if he didn't look like James Dean.

Arresting Cop in *Badlands*

Badlands, a memorable first feature by the 29-year-old Terrence Malick, scored a critical success at the New York Film Festival in 1973. The story was based on the true life events of Charles Stockweather (who was a Dean fan) and Caril Ann Fugate in the mid-1950s.

Holly, a none-too-bright, 15-year-old schoolgirl (Sissy Spacek) fell in love with Kit, a none-too-bright, 25-year-old garbage man (Martin Sheen) because he looked like James Dean. He murdered her father and they went on a killing spree in the Badlands of Dakota and Montana.

The story was related by Holly in the language of teenage romance magazines and what gave the film its special resonance and tensions was the contrast between her matter-of-factness and the terrible events the audience was witnessing on the screen – casual, emotionless, unpremeditated murder of ten innocent people.

'I always wanted to be a criminal, I guess,' said Kit, social misfit and trigger-happy madman, who wanted to be Dean, to have Dean's success, Dean's fame, even Dean's death. At the moment of his capture he behaved like a legendary star and the police and soldiers behaved like adoring fans, eagerly accepting the souvenirs he handed out.

Sheen and Spacek were excellent. Sheen had Dean's hair-style, the same shambling gait and in one scene he adopted the classic crucifix pose with the rifle out of *Giant*. Verbally and in his mannerisms he was Dean.

❝ When I was a young actor in New York there was a saying that if Marlon Brando changed the way actors acted, James Dean changed the way people lived. I believe that.

Martin Sheen

Alive and Well in Argentina

Stage

Writer	Barry Pritchard
Director	Kevin O'Connor
Theatre	St Clements, New York
Date	March 1974

Alive and Well in Argentina, episodic and revue-like, was an absurdist fantasy set in an art deco hotel in South America. The manager was Adolf Hitler, the janitor was James Dean, and the maid was Amelia Earhart. Stephen McHattie played Dean. The critics dismissed the play as aimless and empty.

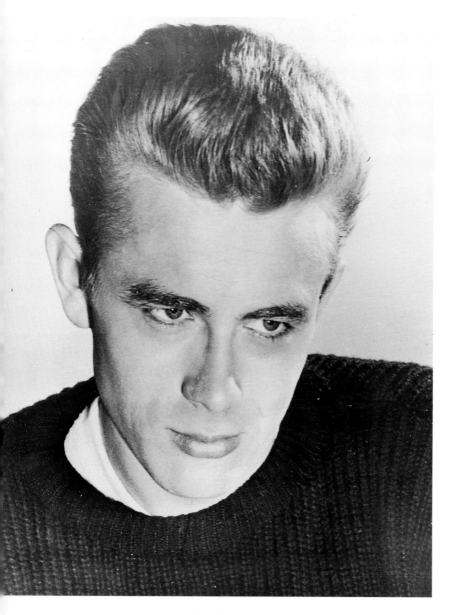

Role	Cast
Bill Bast	Michael Brandon
James Dean	Stephen McHattie
Beverly	Brooke Adams
Ray	Julian Barton
Chris	Candy Clark
James Whitmore	Dane Clark
Dizzy	Meg Foster
Claire Folger	Katherine Helmond
Norma Jean	Amy Irving
Mechanic	Robert Kenton
Reva Randall	Jane Meadows
Jan	Heather Menzies
Judge	Jack Murdock
Mr Robbins	James O'Connell
Arlene	Leland Palmer
Secretary	Chris White

❝ To me the clearest reason for his screen success was that sense of intimacy, compelling warmth and directness that he had on the screen came straight from his private life.

William Bast quoted in *Photoplay*

James Dean: Portrait of a Friend, a 21st anniversary tribute, was an image of the man as seen through the eyes of a friend, intensely personal, elusive and incomplete.

William Bast's screenplay, an affecting and revealing study of their friendship, was written within the artificial framework of Bast talking to a psychiatrist about a dream he had had, a spurious and morbid nightmare, in which Dean was dead and buried and had come back to haunt Bast, accusing him of deserting him.

'How badly do you want to get to the bottom of this?' asked the psychiatrist, not choosing his vocabulary very carefully. There followed a long flashback.

One scene, set in their bedroom, took a surprisingly close look at the relationship. Michael Brandon (Bast) and Stephen McHattie (Dean) played it semi-naked.

James Dean: Portrait of a Friend

Television

Director	Robert Butler
Company	Jozak
Date	19 February 1976
Writer	William Bast
Photography	Frank Stanley
Poducers	William Bast, John Forbes
Executive producers	Gerald L. Isenberg,
	Gerald W. Abrams

134

Dean: Did you ever make it with
       another guy?

Bast: Are you serious?

Dean: I don't mean kid stuff.
      Everybody does that. I mean
      really. Did you?

Bast: Did you?

Dean: Why not?

Bast: Come on. I've known you to
      flatten guys for even joking
      about it.

Dean: No, that was before I was
      committed to my craft.

Bast: What's that go to do with it?

Dean: Grow up, Willie. We're not at
      college any more. This is the
      real thing. This is life and
      that's part of it. You know
      what Stanislavsky says. An
      actor has to be prepared... We
      owe it to our craft to
      experience everything we
      can... Life's too short. I want
      to do it all. Besides you know
      what they say. Don't knock it
      till you try it.

Bast: Are you kidding? I wouldn't
      even know how to go about it,
      if and when I was ready to
      experiment.

Dean: You've got to make certain sacrifices
      for your art.

Clearly Dean was determined not to miss
out on any experience. (As he had said, in a
much quoted line, he wasn't going to go
through life with one hand tied behind his
back.) He persuaded a reluctant Bast to go off
to a gay bar and get picked up.

Despite the intimacy of this scene, there
were those who still thought that the script

was far too cagey in its approach to Dean's
sexual ambivalence. It would have been
interesting to know how far they expected
Bast to go on television in the 1970s.

Portrait of a Friend was as much a portrait
of Bast as it was of Dean. The film ended on a
sentimental note with him deeply regretting
that he had never let Jimmy know how much
he had loved him and placing a copy of
Antoine de Saint-Exupéry's *The Little Prince*
on his grave.

Dean had underlined two sentences in the
book: 'It is only with the heart that one can
see rightly. What is essential is invisible to the
eye.' *The Little Prince* was one of his favourite
stories and earlier in the film Stephen
McHattie had read the passage about the
taming of the fox with its statement, 'You
become responsible for whatever you tame.'

McHatttie, spectacles on the end of his
nose, projected both the warmth and the
aggression of Dean, catching his smile, his
laugh, his sexiness, his physical and vocal
mannerisms.

Bast, in an interview with *Hollywood
Reporter* (whose critic had admired the
performance's 'charismatic intensity')
explained that they had not wanted an actor
to impersonate Dean, but rather an actor
capable of capturing his essence. If they had
wanted a Dean imitation, he said, they would
have tried to get a night club and TV
impersonator like Rich Little.

McHattie not only captured the essence, he
also managed at times to look remarkably like
Dean and his 'concentrated conviction' and
'remarkable impersonation' were praised by
Sylvia Clayton and Peter Lewis writing
respectively in the *Daily* and *Sunday
Telegraph*.

September 30, 1955

Also known as: 9.30.55

Television title: 24 Hours of the Rebel

Film

Director	James Bridges
Studio	Universal
Release	December 1977
Writer	James Bridges
Producer	Jerry Weintraub
Music	Leonard Rosenman
Photography	Gordon Willis

Role	Cast
Jimmy J	Richard Thomas
Melba Lou	Susan Tyrrell
Charlotte	Deborah Benson
Billie Jean	Lisa Blount
Hanley	Thomas Hulce
Frank	Dennis Quaid
Pat	Mary Kai Clark
Eugene	Dennis Christopher
Jimmy's mother	Collin Wilcox

September 30, 1955 was billed as 'The Day That Shook a Generation'. Somewhat surprisingly, it didn't do well at the box office, failing to reach its target audience, and has rarely been seen since. September 30, 1955 was the day James Dean died. The screenplay, based on James Bridges' play, *How Many Times Did You See 'East of Eden'?* described how the news of his death affected Jimmy J, a middle-class Arkansas college student, a fan so absorbed with Dean, and so self-absorbed, that he had turned his life into a movie.

He and his friends tried to communicate with Dean's spirit, first in a ritual on the beach and then in a candlelit ceremony in a darkened room. 'Do you think I am sick, affected, weird?' he asked a friend.

Towards the end of the film he arrived, wearing a white T-shirt, red wind-cheater, blue jeans and boots. He had just seen *Rebel Without a Cause*. (What else?) 'So much of this movie is like my life,' he declared. 'It's incredible. Scene after scene hit home.' He told his girl friend he was going to California:

"I have to go 'cause you see I got to be where he was and I got to talk to his friends and I got to find out about him 'cause you see I never had a hero before, I mean I never had a hero before, I mean I never had anybody I looked up to, somebody I admired like I admired him, somebody who changed my life the way he changed my life."

Jimmy J said he liked Dean in the same way that Dean had liked Plato. It would have been more accurate to say he loved Dean in the same way that Plato had loved Jim Stark.

The girl friend (who had seen *East of Eden* twenty-two times and couldn't imagine a world without Dean) had been badly burned in a prank he had initiated and he felt guilty about her in much the same way that Jim Stark had felt guilty about Plato's death and Cal Trask had felt guilty about Aron's departure for the war in France. He begged her to forgive him.

The whole scene was written and acted in a manner to recall the death-bed scene between Dean and Raymond Massey in *East of Eden*, even to a nurse outside the door, and just in case anybody still hadn't noticed, Jimmy J actually said, 'The whole thing is starting to feel like the last scene in a movie.'

He then rode off on his newly-bought motor-cycle, leaving cinemagoers to wonder if he, too, was going to crash on the highway for the role identification to be complete.

Richard Thomas as Jimmy J gave a sensitive performance and was particularly good in the long and difficult final monologue, helped (as the cinemagoer was) by Leonard Rosenman's tear-jerking theme music from *East of Eden* playing on the soundtrack.

Dean

Musical

Theatre	London Casino
Date	30 August 1977
Writers	John Howlett and Robert Campbell
Director	Robert H. Livingstone
Decor	Terry Parsons
Lighting	Nick Chelton
Dance	Noel Tovey
Producer	Steven Bentinck

Role	**Cast**
James Dean	Glenn Conway
Elia Kazan	
Nicholas Ray	Murray Kash
George Stevens	
Pier Angeli	
Natalie Wood	Anna Nicholas
Elizabeth Taylor	

James Dean in *Giant*

The production was notable for its problems during rehearsals. The director, the musical director, a leading actor, and the producer all resigned. Terrance Robay, an American rock singer, who had been engaged to play Dean, was sacked.

The book was soft-centred, humourless and cliché-ridden. ('Broadway's not enough, Sam! I want more!') It concentrated on Dean's habit of walking out of shows, his affair with Pier Angeli, and a recreation of scenes from his films: Cal Trask bursting in on his mother in the brothel from *East of Eden* and Plato's death from *Rebel Without a Cause*.

The whole action took place in a film studio. The music was pastiche 1950s rock. The lyrics were largely inaudible. The staging was efficient. The high spot was the show's climax: the oil-well in *Giant* exploding into a cascade of gold sparks.

Glenn Conway, a personable lookalike, with a fine strong voice, had Dean's slouch, vulnerable smile, springy walk, hunched shoulders, and the unenviable task of recreating Dean's acting. His solo numbers included titles like, 'I Scream', 'Running Out of Time', and 'Misery, Misery'.

The show, which opened to better reviews than might have been expected, closed after five weeks, and resurfaced Off-Broadway some time later in a miniature version.

" Dean always arrived looking unwashed and scruffy. He'd wear old jeans, which the kids did not do then, lie back on the couch and put his feet up. We told him to get out. He was always making a nuisance of himself.

Rose Tobias, casting director of *Dean*

Come Back to the 5 and Dime, Jimmy Dean, Jimmy Dean

Stage and Screen

Theatre	Martin Beck, New York*
Date	18 February 1982
Writer	Ed Graczyk
Director	Robert Altman
Scenery	David Gropman
Lighting	Paul Gallo

Role	**Cast**
Juanita	Sudie Bond
Sissy	Cher
Mona	Sandy Dennis
Joe	Mark Patton
Sue Ellen	Gena Ramsel
Stella Mae	Kathy Bates
Edna Louise	Marta Heflin
Martha	Ann Risley
Alice Ann	Dianne Turley Travis
Clarissa	Ruth Miller
Joanna	Karen Black

Come Back to the 5 and Dime, Jimmy Dean, Jimmy Dean was originally produced Off-Broadway at Hudson Guild Theater on 27 February 1980.

The Disciples of James Dean gathered for a reunion on the 20th anniversary of his death in a small town Texas store filled with Dean memorabilia and run by a Christian fundamentalist.

Ed Graczyk's play was in the William Inge manner, a saga of unfulfilled dreams and a lot of chatter by a quintet of immature middle-aged women. The action alternated between 30 September 1975 and 30 September 1955.

Robert Altman transferred his stage production to the screen in 19 days without disguising its stage origins. He made clever use of a wall-size mirror so that the two time scales could be played concurrently.

Mona (more like a character out of a play by Tennessee Williams) had pretended for 20 years, though nobody had believed her, that her illegitimate son had been fathered by James Dean when she was an extra on *Giant*. The father was in fact Joe, a gay boy, who had left town, had a sex change, and now returned for the first time as Joanna. Karen Black brilliantly suggested the male body inside the female form. She looked like a man in drag.

Mark Patton played young Joe, a character who like the women's younger selves, lived now only in their imaginations. His son, a much-talked-about rebel given to fast driving, never appeared.

James Dean, A Dress Rehearsal

Stage

Writer	Patricia A. Leone
Director	Patricia A. Leone
Theatre	45th Street Theater New York
Date	1984

James Dean, A Dress Rehearsal (originally produced in Denver, Colorado) was in two acts.

In the first act Dean was rehearsing a play and misbehaving according to legend: a volatile personality frustrating the other actors and being reprimanded by the director.

In the second act he was at a press conference fielding questions about his sexual life by a woman from *The New York Times* and a sportswriter.

Patricia Leone and Stephen Brannan (who played Dean) both got poor reviews.

139

Awards

Fairmount High School

1949 The Madman's Manuscript from Charles Dickens's The Pickwick Papers

National Forensic League Speech Competition
Indiana State Contest: *First Place*
National Contest: *Sixth Place*

Theatre

1954 The Immoralist

The Daniel Blum Theater World Award:
Most Promising Personalty (one of 12 actors to win the award)

Film

1955 East of Eden

The American Academy of Motion Pictures Arts and Sciences
Oscar nomination: *Best Actor*

Hollywood Foreign Press Association Golden Globe Award:
Special Posthumous Award

Film Daily
Award: *Best Performance by a Male Star*
Award: *Finds of the Year*

Motion Picture Exhibitors
Award: *Stars of Tomorrow*

Photoplay Gold Medal
Award: *Special Achievement*

Modern Screen Silver Cup
Award: *Special Achievement*

James Dean in *Giant*

British Academy
Award: *Best Foreign Actor*

Picturegoer
Award: *Best Actor*

The Crystal Star (France)
Award: *Best Actor*

Audience Awards Election
Award: *Best Actor*

1955 Rebel Without a Cause

National Association of Theater Owners
Award: *Best Actor*

The Yokohama Movie Circle Council
Award: *Best Male Star*

The Million Pearl Award (Japan)
Award: *Best Foreign Actor*

The Tokyo Movie Fan's Association
Award: *Top Foreign Actor*

1956 Giant

The American Academy of Motion Pictures Arts and Sciences
Oscar nomination: *Best Actor*

Hollywood Foreign Press Association Golden Globe Award:
World Film Favourite

New York Film Critics
Award: *Best Actor Runner-Up*

Film Daily
Award: *Best Supporting Actor*

Winged Victor Award (France)
Award: *Best Actor 1957*

Chronology

Theatre

Amateur Actor at School

Date	Title	Role
1945	To Them That Sleep in Darkness	Blind Boy
1946	The Monkey's Paw	Herbert White
	An Apple From Coles County	Not identified
1947	Mooncalf Mugford	John Mugford
	Our Hearts Were Young and Gay	Otis Skinner
1948	Goon with the Wind	Villain and Frankenstein's monster
1949	You Can't Take it with You	Boris Kalenkhov
	'The Madman's Manuscript'	Madman

Amateur Actor at College and University

Date	Title	Role
1949	The Romance of Scarlet Gulch	Charlie Smooch
1950	She Was Only A Farmer's Daughter	Father
	Iz Zat So? (a revue)	Various
	Macbeth	Malcolm

Actors Studio and Professional Actor in New York

Date	Title	Role
1952	Matador	Matador
	The Metamorphosis*	Ensemble
	See The Jaguar	Wally Wilkins
1953	End as a Man**	Cadet
	The Seagull**	Konstantin Treplev
	The Scarecrow	Scarecrow's image
	Aria Da Capo**	Pierrot
	The Fell Swoop*	Not identified
1954	The Immoralist	Bachir
	Women of Trachis*	Herakles

Television

Date	Title	Role
1951	Hill Number One	John the Apostle
	T.K.O.	Not identified
1952	Into the Valley	GI
	Sleeping Dogs	Vagrant
	Ten Thousand Horses Singing	Bellhop
	The Foggy, Foggy Dew	Kyle McCallum
	Prologue to Glory	Denny
	Abraham Lincoln	William Scott
	The Forgotten Children	Bradford
1953	The Hound of Heaven	Angel
	The Case of the Watchful Dog	Randy Meeker
	The Killing of Jesse James	Bob Ford
	No Room	Safe-cracker
	The Case of the Sawed-Off Shotgun	Arbie Ferris
	The Evil Within	Ralph
	Something for an Empty Briefcase	Joe Adams
	Sentence of Death	Joe Palica
	Death Is My Neighbor	JB
	Rex Newman	Not identified
	Glory in the Flower	Bronco
	Keep Our Honor Bright	Jim
	Life Sentence	Hank Bradon
	A Long Time Till Dawn	Joe Harris
	The Bells of Cockaigne	Joey
	Harvest	Paul Zalenka
1954	The Little Woman	Augie
	Run Like a Thief	Rob
	Padlock	Felon
	I'm a Fool	The Boy
	The Dark, Dark Hour	Delinquent
1955	The Thief	Fernand Lagarde
	The Unlighted Road	Jeff Latham

*staged readings

**Actors Studio in-house performances

Television Commercials

Date	Company
1950	Pepsi–Cola
1955	National Safety Council

Film

Date	Title	Role
1951	Fixed Bayonets!	GI
	Sailor Beware!	Boxer's second
1952	Has Anybody Seen My Gal	College student
1955	East of Eden	Cal Trask
	Rebel Without a Cause	Jim Stark
1956	Giant	Jett Rink

Documentaries

Date	Title	Director
1956	The Steve Allen Show	Steve Allen
1957	The James Dean Story	Robert Altman
1975	James Dean – The First American Teenager (Alternative title: Idol – the Story of James Dean)	Ray Connolly
1982	Hollywood: I Rebelli 'James Dean' (English title: Hollywood: The Rebels 'James Dean')	Claudio Masenza
1988	Forever James Dean	Ara Cheymayan
1990	Bye Bye Jimmy	Paul Watson
1997	James Dean: The Race With Destiny	Mardi Rustan

Related Works

Date	Title	Description
1958	The Myth Makers	Television
1962	To Climb Steep Hills	Television
	The Movie Star	Television
1974	Badlands	Film
	Alive and Well in Argentina	Theatre
1976	James Dean: Portrait of a Friend	Television
1977	September 30, 1955	Film
	Dean	Theatre (musical)
1982	Come Back to the 5 and Dime, Jimmy Dean, Jimmy Dean	Theatre and Film
1984	James Dean, A Dress Rehearsal	Theatre

Acknowledgements

Robert Tanitch would like to begin by expressing his appreciation to his editor, Richard Reynolds, and designers, Paul Tavener, text, and Daniel Duke, cover.

The author and publisher would like to express their appreciation to the following for their assistance and/or permission in relation to the following photographs: British Film Institute: 11,57, 79, 81, 82, 85, 87, 90, 97, 101, 105, 108, 111, 112, 113, 134, 137. Joel Finler: 8, 12, 76, 89, 95, 96, 102, 119, 127, 129, 131, 138. The David Loehr Collection, The James Dean Gallery, Fairmount: 7, 17, 18, 24, 26, 29, 31, 34, 47, 59, 66, 72.

Robert Tanitch would like to express his appreciation to The New York Museum of Television and Radio for enabling him to watch James Dean's television work and in particular to Jennifer Lewis, Jonathan Rosenthall, Ron Simon, and Robert Scott and his staff, for all their valuable help. He would like to thank: everybody at the British Film Institute, reference library, stills and viewing departments; everybody at the Westminster Central Library; everybody at the Billy Rose Theatre Collection at the New York Library; and everybody at the Theatre Museum, London.

He would also like to express his thanks to: David Loehr and Lenny at The James Dean Gallery in Fairmount, Indiana, USA; Geraldine Duclow, Head of Theatre Collection Free Library of Philadlephia; and to William Bast, Sylvia Bongiovanni, Maryam Chach, Jel Finler, Peter Hirst, Gladys Irvis, Haydn Smith, and Stuart McCready.

Index